A Delicate
and Difficult Question

Documents in the History
of Ukrainians in Canada
1899 - 1962

A Delicate
and Difficult Question

Documents in the History
of Ukrainians in Canada
1899 - 1962

Bohdan S. Kordan
Lubomyr Y. Luciuk

THE LIMESTONE PRESS
Kingston — Ontario
1986

BUILDERS OF CANADA SERIES
No. 3
Series Editor
Richard A. Pierce
Professor of History, Queen's University

CANADIAN CATALOGUING IN PUBLICATION DATA
Main entry under title:
A delicate and difficult question: documents
in the history of Ukrainians in Canada, 1899-1962

(Builders of Canada; no. 3)
Bibliography: p.
ISBN 0-919642-08-X

1. Ukrainians—Canada—History—Sources.
I. Kordan, Bohdan S.   II. Luciuk, Lubomyr Y.,
1953-   III. Series: Builders of Canada
(Kingston, Ont.); no. 3.

FC106.U5D44 1986   971'.00491791   C86-090154-8
   F1035.U5D44 1986

Typesetting by
Multilingual on Whyte
Printed in Canada by
Brown and Martin Ltd.

The Limestone Press
Box 1604
Kingston, Ontario
K7L 5C8

For J. E. Tracy Philipps
(1890-1959)

Preface

Preparing a documentary collection involves selecting materials to illustrate the main themes being addressed. This work is concerned with the nature of Ukrainian identity in Canada, and how this allegiance has been shaped and influenced through the maintenance of group ties with the European homeland and interaction in North America with the host society and the Canadian state. It also touches on the question of how competing perceptions of what it means to be a Ukrainian in Canada have developed. Fundamentally, it is our contention that the state's role in shaping the nature of ethnic identity is far more salient than has been previously recognized. Although the state has never made an effort to proscribe Ukrainian culture in Canada, it has — especially in times of crisis — taken steps to channel this minority's political behaviour into acceptable forms. Its surveillance of the group and sporadic interventions have signalled the government's unwillingness to accept any encroachment on its domestic and foreign policy prerogatives. While this ethnic community has demonstrated a great deal of adaptability, it nevertheless has been worn down and altered through its unequal interaction with the state and its own internal divisiveness.

Fifty-five documents are contained in this collection, covering the period 1899-1962. Declassified government materials comprise the core of the work although a number of pivotal editorials from the Ukrainian language press in Canada and programmatic statements made by organizations are also included in translation. These documents have been selected because they represent identifiable currents and trends which have worked interactively to shape the nature of Ukrainian identity in Canada. They imply the need for the development of a theoretical framework within which the historical pattern of this ethnic group's experience can be understood.

The majority of the documents are drawn from public and private archives from across North America. With few exceptions, this material has never been published before. Every attempt has been made to preserve the essence of the original statements or reports. A number of the documents, however, have been abridged due to their length. Passages which have been omitted are identified by elipses marks [........]. The occasional illegible word was marked as follows: [_____]. The language of original text is English unless identified otherwise. An introduction has been included to provide the reader with a concise overview of the Ukrainian experience in Canada; the narrative closely follows the documents cited in this collection. The intention of the annotations which accompany the documents is to place each in a precise historical context.

The collection ends with the year 1962. This is not an arbitrary cut-off point. Rather it stems from restrictions which have prevented the further release of government documents from the period following this date. Documents within the collection are skewed toward the later years. This is the result of there being greater political activity within a more mature organized community.

The authors thank the Archives of Ontario, the History Section of the Canadian Department of External Affairs, Hoover Institution Archives, Public Archives of Canada, United States National Archives, Social Sciences and Humanities Research Council of Canada, Messrs. M. Bartkiw, W. Bezchlibnyk, M. Carynnyk, D. Cole, J. Kolasky, D. Lupul, E. Martel, M. Momryk, Ms. I. Mycak, G. B. Panchuk, A. Papanek, B. Rankin, Dr. O. Romany-shyn, A. Rutkowski, Y. Weretelnyk, and Professors P. Magosci and R. Franko.

This book would not have been possible without the financial support of the Prometheus Foundation, Ukrainian Canadian Committee, Ukrainian Canadian Veteran's Association, Ukrainian Branches of the Royal Canadian Legion (Edmonton, Winnipeg, Toronto, Montreal), the Chair of Ukrainian Studies at the University of Toronto, Ucrainica Research Institute, Canadian League for the Liberation of Ukraine, and the Multiculturalism Directorate, Secretary of State.

Heartfelt thanks are extended to Professor Richard Pierce, editor of The Limestone Press, for taking on this project.

Bohdan S. Kordan   Lubomyr Y. Luciuk
                    Kingston, 1986

Contents

Introduction:

The Ukrainian Experience in Canada

Hiving together in rural bloc settlements on the prairies and far removed from the political heartland of Canada, the immigrant mass which had migrated primarily from Ukrainian ethnographic territories in eastern Europe between 1891-1914 collectively faced the hardships of homesteading. In this period, over 170,000 individuals from the regions of Galicia, Bukovyna and Transcarpathia were allowed into Canada. It was a veritable exodus which said as much about the conditions left behind in their homeland as it did about the expected promise of Canada. From their experiences a group consciousness would crystalize among this formerly unconsolidated mass, a process catalyzed through interaction with the dominant and assimilationist Anglo-Celtic population of Canada. Within a span of one generation, these immigrants began to acquire a collective sense of identity which led to a rediscovery of a more formal historical past and a closer association with the larger Ukrainian nation in Europe. It was a logical step in the formative process of ethnic identification because, as these settlers and labourers themselves came to appreciate, their shared social experience as an oppressed people in eastern Europe was simply a reflection of their status in Canada.

What these immigrants failed to realize, however, was that this condition was a consequence of Canada's own nation-building policy. Clifford Sifton, Interior Minister in the Laurier government, argued for and successfully implemented a policy which introduced the Ukrainian peasant as a unique and cheap economic factor in the development of the Canadian hinterland (No. 1). The introduction of Ukrainians into the social structure generated a heated and far-ranging policy debate on the future character of Canadian society (No. 2), a debate which would carry on in the public forum well into the 1920s (No. 14). Political considerations aside, Sifton understood that the economics of western growth would depend on tying agriculturalists to the land. Since the Ukrainian peasantry had demonstrated an ability to operate under adverse conditions, Sifton deemed them to be the most suitable as an immigrant stock (No. 1). For Ukrainians, on the other hand, their entry status into the Canadian social structure as a rural labouring class would retard the material development of the community and condition the character of their early social and political life in Canada (No. 5).

Understandably, Ukrainians desired to change their status, and their efforts took two principal forms. One was based on a class orientation; the other focussed more exclusively on ethnic and national identity. Identification with class struggle, however, did not preclude ethnic affiliation and the result was the formation of radical political organizations which were decidedly Ukrainian in character (No. 3). As for those who no longer found the issue of class struggle relevant but who still coalesced around the issue of their identity, they became increasingly active in promoting and encouraging the cultural, educational, and economic welfare of the community. They professed the liberal view that only a self-reliant and intellectually prepared individual could deal with the realities of the economic marketplace (No. 4), and emphasized the logical connection between the historic struggle of the Ukrainian nation in Europe and the struggle of the Ukrainian ethnic group in Canada to maintain its integrity and identity. Steps were taken to reinforce that natural link. Encouraged by parallel developments in Ukraine, for example, a national Ukrainian church and affiliated lay body in Canada were created in 1918 to serve the needs of a growing nationally conscious community (No. 8, No. 9). More importantly, however, among those who were developing this nationalist perspective, there emerged a sincere belief that Canadian liberal democracy would enable them to give succor to the homeland to which their ethnicity bound them. What they failed to recognize was that the state would not permit them to shape their own ethnic and political space within Canada if this process were to present serious challenges to state authority.

Between 1917 and 1921, war and revolution in eastern Europe provided the setting for the national and class options to be played out on Ukrainian territories. During this period several unsuccessful attempts were made at establishing an independent Ukrainian national state, the most important of which was the Ukrainian Democratic Republic. In the aftermath of hostilities, however, it was the Ukrainian Soviet Socialist Republic which was formed under Soviet Russian hegemony. In Canada, this latter development was to hearten the Ukrainian-Canadian Left which saw in this newly created state the promise of a better life for their kindred in the homeland and a political entity that would champion the cause of the international proletariat. On the other hand, nationally-minded Ukrainians, who had petitioned Canadian authorities to intervene actively in favour of the republican forces (No. 11), were dismayed. The collapse of the republic meant the further colonialization of Ukraine. Moreover, the future of the nationalist community in Canada would continue to be discouraging, if not difficult and tenuous since there would not be a clearly identified national state to legitimize their position as Canadians of Ukrainian origin (No. 13).

The Great War of 1914-1918 was to have further implications for Ukrainian Canadians. Exasperated by the demands of war, xenophobes would portray Ukrainians as a people of divided loyalties. The initial cause for suspicion and accusation — despite a quick retraction (No. 7) — was provided by Bishop Budka's pastoral letter of July 27, 1914 (No. 6). The letters would set a tone for the duration of the war as the Canadian state's internal security system targeted Ukrainian nationalists and radicals alike. The politically innocent who were unfortunate enough to be suspect simply because of their nationality also became victims of the state's security apparatus. Between the years 1914-1920, thousands were registered as enemy aliens, and some 8,500 individuals were interned. Ukrainians constituted the largest proportion, comprising the majority of the 6,000 "Austrian" nationals who were imprisoned. Their disenfranchisement as enemy aliens under the War-time Election Act of 1917 also added to the collective humiliation as some 143,000 Ukrainians were affected.

Internment operations demonstrated the extent to which Ottawa was prepared to use force to guarantee its nation-building prerogatives despite objections by elected officials who viewed the overall actions of the state as detrimental to the long-term interests of Canada (No. 10). Even after the war, there were those in the highest circles who advocated the use af state terror during labour unrest to subdue once and for all the ethnic labour element in Canada (No. 12). The internment experience and the knowledge that force could be used arbitrarily were to have a decisive influence on the manner in which Ukrainians were to perceive their relationship to the state and the way they would articulate their identity in the future. Some twenty years later, for example, an RCMP operative commenting on the nationalist leadership of the Ukrainian-Canadian community noted the sobering effect that the "fear of the barbed wire fence" had on their political outlook.

The internment experience, deportations and the set-backs suffered by the labour movement in the years following the war contributed to the hardening of the position of the Ukrainian-Canadian Left. By the late 1920s, in keeping with Comintern directives which called for intensification of the class struggle, cadres were apparently sent from the Ukrainian Labour-Farmer Temple Association (ULFTA) — the largest Ukrainian left-wing mass organization — to the Soviet Union for training in agitation and underground work (No. 17, No. 18). However, the demand by the Canadian Communist party leadership for greater participation of the ULFTA rank-and-file in the labour struggles as well as the pressure to eliminate the "national exclusiveness" of Ukrainian mass organizations (No. 19) created a rift between the Politburo of the Communist Party of Canada (CPC) and the Ukrainian leadership in the party. The Ukrainian contingent rejected the Politburo's criticism of "bourgeois deviationism" and claimed that the ULFTA had the right to maintain its autonomous political and national character (No. 20). Under pressure to follow party policy as formulated and directed by the Politburo, a secret Ukrainian caucus met in 1930 to discuss breaking away from the CPC. Fearing a mass defection of Ukrainians from both the party and other left-wing organizations, the Politburo retreated from its original position, and a permanent split in the Ukrainian-Canadian Left was temporarily averted.

In the nationalist camp, opinion was divided over whether support for the idea of a sovereign Ukrainian state was compatible with their civic obligations as Canadian citizens. The conundrum was resolved through the argument that Ukrainian Canadians could advance the interests of the Ukrainian nation in Europe only by demonstrating loyalty to the British Crown. This belief was based on the perception that the Ukrainian immigration which had come to Canada did so with the view of building a new life.

Therefore, its primary allegiance was to the adopted homeland. This did not mean having to abandon the idea of an independent Ukraine, but rather as a political question that goal would be resolved by events in Europe. Nevertheless, Ukrainian-Canadian nationalists believed that their views on the issue of Ukrainian sovereignty would be heard if they participated unambiguously in the social and political mainstream as loyal Canadian citizens (No. 16). This position became the ideological cornerstone of the programme of the Ukrainian Self-Reliance League (No. 15).

Significantly, this formula — to be a good Ukrainian one had to be a good Canadian — was given new meaning when the Governor General of Canada, Lord Tweedsmuir, in an appearance before a Ukrainian audience in 1936, stated that to be a good Canadian one first had to be a good Ukrainian (No. 24). His inversion of the equation was to hearten Ukrainian-Canadian nationalists as well as comfort future generations of Ukrainian Canadians, who would turn to the statement for vindication of their ethnicity.

The situation within the interwar period was to be complicated by the immigration of nationally conscious Ukrainians to Canada during the years 1925-30. The approximately 58,000 Ukrainian immigrants who arrived from Europe at this time were, for the most part, witnesses to the social and political upheavals which enveloped their homeland during the years 1917-21. Although not political refugees in the strict sense, a significant portion of this immigrant wave supported and sympathized with the defeated republican movement. Among its more militant elements, the belief emerged that only an independent Ukrainian national state would present Ukrainians with the opportunity to develop both socially and politically. Armed with this conviction, they sought to mobilize the community and elevate it above what were perceived to be rather narrow religious and party concerns; the ideal of creating a Ukrainian national state would take priority over all other obligations.

Their efforts elicited a strong reaction from the more moderate nationalists, most notably the Ukrainian Self-Reliance League, who believed that the uncompromising position of this element threatened to jeopardize the recent social gains made by the already established Ukrainian community in Canada.

Various international developments in the 1930s, such as the rise of revisionist powers in Europe, the Polish "pacification" of western Ukraine and the Great Famine of 1932-1933 in Soviet Ukraine were also to influence the character of the organized Ukrainian-Canadian community. For example, news of the 1933 famine, generated within the nationalist community politically non-partisan appeals to foreign heads of state to alleviate the plight of the Ukrainian people (No. 22, No. 23). Reports of the Stalinist terror also forced Ukrainian dissidents within the Communist party to criticize the leadership and leave both the party and its affiliate, the ULFTA (No. 25). Never abandoning their commitment to the labour movement, this minority was to gravitate toward the national camp, and their arrival eventually enabled a coalition of interests to emerge that was centrist in character. This moderate Centre, however, was viewed with suspicion by the more militant Ukrainian-Canadian nationalists. Disenchanted with the inability of international organizations such as the League of Nations to deal with the question of national and minority rights and buoyed by the prospect of a geopolitical restructuring of Europe by the revisionist powers of Germany and Italy, this element became more vocal in its opposition to the international *status quo* (No. 21). The result was the polarization of the organized Ukrainian-Canadian community. On one extreme stood the ULFTA, which committed itself to Leninist orthodoxy and a pro-Soviet line. On the other extreme were the Ukrainian National Federation (UNF) and the United Hetman Organization (UHO), which articulated nationalist and monarchist views, respectively. The Right managed to

escape severe censure only because it was careful not to place
itself in direct opposition to the Canadian state (No. 21).

Everything was to change in 1939; the year marked a
critical watershed in Ukrainian-Canadian history. The active collaboration of the Soviet Union with Nazi Germany
allowed Ukrainian-Canadian nationalists to argue that the
security of the British Empire could only be enhanced by the
creation of an independent Ukraine and that the new international alignment, which witnessed the liberal democracies
pitted against totalitarianism, created an ethical climate
which favoured Ukrainian independence (No. 26). Moreover, the call by the Canadian Communist party demanding
Canada's withdrawal from the "imperialist war" and the
state's reaction — including internment of party members,
the outlawing of the ULFTA, and confiscation of its properties — led Ukrainian-Canadian nationalists to believe that
the political lines were now clearly drawn in their favour.
The stage appeared to be set as the confluence of interests
provided a historically unprecedented situation; Ukrainian
independence was almost assured. This, however, was not
to be realized despite attempts within the Ukrainian-
Canadian nationalist community to make certain that the
issue of Ukrainian sovereignty was heard (No. 27).

Britain's commitment to the inviolability of Poland's
pre-1939 boundaries, which included western Ukrainian territories, and the view that the integrity of the Soviet Union
as a political entity had to be maintained if British political
and military options were to remain open meant that Britain
would not encourage Ukrainian national aspirations.
Canada was unprepared to break with Britain's lead on the
question; in Ottawa's view, the demands of total war and
Canadian foreign policy far outweighed the importance of
support for an independent Ukraine. Ukrainian-Canadian
nationalist activity, therefore, was soon to be viewed with
suspicion, prompting surveillance of the community's
organizations (No. 31). Such activity also forced state

authorities to take some preliminary steps in dissipating tension over the issue. With the active intervention of the
government, the Ukrainian Canadian Committee (UCC)
was created in 1940 (No. 28). The idea was that this
organization would fulfill the short-term objectives of rally-
ing Ukrainian-Canadian public opinion behind the war effort while simultaneously dampening any inimical behaviour. Ironically, though perhaps not unexpectedly, the UCC
actively began to express the expectations of the Ukrainian-
Canadian nationalist community (No. 36). Notwithstanding
its desire to co-operate with Canadian authorities, the UCC
also came under official surveillance (No. 37).

The potential status that the UCC might have developed as a spokesbody for the nationalist camp was never
realized. By mid-1941, the USSR was forced to join the
Anglo-American alliance. As a result, the UCC was
suddenly emasculated and thereafter would expend its
energies largely in conflict with a renascent Left (No. 29)
while defensively arguing the question of Ukraine's right to
national self-determination.

Discord between the Left and Right and the potential
that the issue of Ukrainian independence had in creating
further divisions in public opinion (No.32) signaled to state
officials the need for policy in dealing with the problem.
These authorities were also motivated in their concern
because of international considerations. The Americans,
who viewed their security in hemispheric terms, looked
askance at Ottawa's handling of the entire matter and began
their own surveillance of the Ukrainian situation in Canada
(No. 39). On the other hand, the Soviets were openly critical
and outraged that Canadian authorities would tolerate
elements which ostensibly advocated the breakup of an ally
(No. 33). The Ukrainian problem, in effect, threatened
Canada's role as a "responsible" international actor,
necessitating the development of a policy to deal with the
community. Once the parameters of the policy were defined

(No. 35), its directives were immediately put into practice. Canadian government officials, however, also asked for patience from their critics, especially the Soviet Union, whose objections, they felt, only served to aggravate the situation in Canada (No. 43). In the final analysis, senior Canadian officials believed that the Ukrainian problem would disappear of its own accord (No. 42).

By the concluding phase of the war, the UCC did present, in fact, a much muted public position on the issue of Ukrainian independence. Even the militant UNF had, by 1945, retreated to join the political Centre. All the constituent groups associated with the UCC conceded that the liberation struggle would have to be carried on primarily by those in the homeland with, at best, moral support from Ukrainians in Canada (No. 44). This modified position, however, did not prevent the UCC from participating in relief efforts to alleviate the plight of countless hundreds of thousands of Ukrainians who were left displaced because of the turbulent events of the war (No. 40, No. 41). Nor did it preclude them from intervening on humanitarian grounds when the issue of resettling Ukrainian displaced persons (DPs) in Europe arose (No. 45).

Ukrainian-Canadian expectations about the role a new wave of Ukrainian immigrants would have within organized community life were not all met. The Ukrainian-Canadian Left argued for a selective immigration policy which they felt would be in keeping with Canada's long-term economic strategy of industrial and agricultural expansion (No. 46). The emphasis on admitting only workers and farmers was predicated, ostensibly, on the assumption that class identification would favour the labour movement in Canada. Furthermore, it was assumed that an influx of Ukrainian workers would replenish the ranks of Ukrainian left-wing organizations. Ironically, the new Ukrainian immigration, which in its class composition consisted almost entirely of workers and peasants, was to become the most vehement critic of the Ukrainian-Canadian Left. Confronted by these witnesses who could speak to the reality of Stalinist rule in Soviet Ukraine, membership in the already diminishing Ukrainian left-wing organizations declined precipitously.

Significantly, many of the new refugees, as exponents of a militant Ukrainian nationalism (No. 47), also found themselves in disagreement with those who seemed content with building a Ukrainian community in Canada. For those who were intent on returning to the homeland, this Ukrainian-Canadian emphasis on remaining in what many DPs deemed to be only a place of temporary asylum was unacceptable (No. 50). This attitude had the practical effect of insulating the major political organization established by Ukrainian refugees, the Canadian League for the Liberation of Ukraine. The organization was to operate and remain outside the established Ukrainian-Canadian community structure for more than ten years (No. 53). However, the prospect of remaining indefinitely in Canada generated serious internal debate within the leadership of the organization (No. 50) and eventually led to an uneasy compromise with the UCC.

The political activity of the post-war immigrants imparted a renewed vigour to the UCC's ability to lobby the Canadian government on a variety of questions including that of Ukrainian independence (No. 48). Paradoxically, given the international political climate of the Cold War, these representations were never acted upon as their bearers had anticipated. Instead, the government developed a standard response which dismissed all such petitions (No. 49, No. 52). It also outlined an official position which categorically rejected the historical, legal, and political claims of Ukrainians to independence (No. 51, No. 55) and communicated this position to other foreign governments which expressed a similar interest in the issue (No. 54).

Canada's gatekeepers had allowed Ukrainian immigrants into Canada primarily to serve the nation-building needs of the state. Faced with the emergence of a Ukrainian identity in Canada as well as radical Ukrainian-Canadian organizations of the Left and Right, it acted forcefully only when international crises dictated the need for some concomitant domestic action. These actions were rationalized through what were perceived to be the state's nation-building prerogatives. In the main, however, officials were content to leave organized Ukrainian society in Canada undisturbed. Since competing visions of what it meant to be Ukrainian in Canada would grind down the Ukrainian-Canadian community, it appeared that the passage of time itself would be sufficient to eliminate what Norman Robertson, the dean of the Canadian diplomatic service, once described as this most "delicate and difficult question."

Documents

*The influx of Ukrainian immigrants into the Canadian West
at the turn of the century provoked a national controversy. Clifford
Sifton, the Minister of Interior, defended the Laurier government's
immigration policies on the basis of economic necessity. Critics,
however, argued for responsible policy, claiming that economic considerations aside, the process of nation-building had a social di-
mension with long-term consequences which could not be ignored.*

No. 1: Commons Debates, July 7, 1899, Concerning Ukrainian Immigration

FOREIGN IMMIGRATION

[........]

THE MINISTER OF THE INTERIOR: [........] As to the ques-
tion of the desirability of these settlers generally, I will take up just for a
few minutes two or three objections that have been raised. In the first
place, I desire to say that the hon. member for Victoria, B.C., (Mr. Prior)
is not correct when he says there is any disposition on the part of the con-
tinental settlers, the Galicians and Doukhobors, to come to the towns.
That is not correct. These people have no disposition for an urban life.
Once they get into such a position on land that they have enough to eat
and a house to live in, they have no disposition to go to the cities. Their
habits are altogether the other way, and that is one of the prime reasons
why I thought it desirable not to discourage unduly their immigration. If
these people were people not accustomed to agricultural life, with any
disposition at all to abandon agricultural life and come to the towns, I
would unhesitatingly use every power that the Government would place in
my hands for the purpose of preventing their going to the North-west, for
nothing but disaster would result from such a course; but it is because
these people are agriculturists and have been for generations, because they
have no idea of following any life except that of agriculturists, because
their one idea is to go on land and stay there, that I consider them unques-
tionably good agricultural settlers and an acquisition to the country. These
people came in at first under rather unfortunate auspices. While I do not
wish to make a party discussion out of this I am bound to say the late
Government was somewhat to blame for those unfortunate auspices. The
movement began under the late Government. Professor Oleskow came
out here and interviewed the Minister of the Interior of that day and the
officers of that department. Having had a special authority from the
Austrian Government in connection with the matter, he was desirous of

making an arrangement whereby he would be authorized, for a certain payment, to supervise the immigration of the Galicians. The Government of that day did not see fit to make any arrangement with him, but these people came in just the same. The result was, that no supervision and no care was exercised in their selection, and the people who did come in at first were the least desirable of all the Galicians that have come to the country. Professor Oleskow informs us that if he had been employed to exercise any degree of supervision, the people who first came and who were the people that went to Edmonton and who first gave rise to the unalterable hostility which the hon. member for Alberta (Mr. Oliver) has against the Galicians, would probably not have come at all. They were just such people as can be picked up in any country — paupers where they came from, and, of course, paupers when they got here. Since arriving, however, they have done fairly well. That does not, however, at all apply to the Galicians generally that have been coming in since. I may say to my hon. friend that one of the first matters called to my attention, on assuming office, was, that there were a couple of Galician settlements not doing well, for the reason that they had been given no direction or assistance in the way of advice as to the methods of conducting operations in this country, and consequently some of them had got discouraged and gone into the town, just as my hon. friend suggested they had a disposition to do. But they did not go into the town because they had a disposition to do so, but because they had been turned loose on the country, without any instructions being given them as to the methods to be followed, so that they did not know what to do, and became totally discouraged. But what I did in connection with these people was this. I consulted my chief officers of immigration; we went over the whole case, and the result was, that, of the 115 Galicians who were in Winnipeg when I took office, at the end of six months after my immigration commissioner took charge of the work, there were not five. All had moved out to the Stuartburn settlement, where they are prosperous today, and under no obligations to anybody. The difficulty in their case at first was simply because they were dumped into the country and no attention whatever paid to them. But those people are now upon their feet in the Stuartburn settlement, not far south-east of Winnipeg. The settlement is a prosperous one, and the people there are doing quite as well as a lot of people coming from a foreign country, under similar circumstances, could possibly be expected to do. There is no movement of these people to the towns in the slightest degree. On the contrary, they manifest the strongest disinclination to the town, and a determination to stay on their land and make homes for themselves, if possible.

So far as the Galicians are concerned, the attacks that have been made upon them, in my judgment, are most unfair and most ungenerous.

If we are ever going to have the North-west populated, we shall not succeed in doing it by standing on our boundary with a club or putting the
microscope on every man who wishes to come into the country. We have
had these prairies for a good many years now. I have seen the towns and
cities in the North-west with business stagnant, and business people leaving them, and everybody in the North-west getting discouraged, because
the urban population had nothing to do. And why? Simply because there
were no people to trade with. The only solution of our problem there, is to
get people on the land who will till it. And I am prepared to say this: That
I do not care what language a man speaks, or what religion he professes, if
he is honest and law-abiding, if he will go on the land and make a living
for himself and family, he is a desirable settler for the Dominion of
Canada; and the people of Canada will never succeed in populating
Manitoba and the North-west until we act practically upon that idea. And
upon the development of Manitoba and the North-west, in my judgment,
the future greatness and prosperity of this Dominion of Canada very
largely depends. In so saying, I do not wish to minimize the importance of
other parts of the country, but I think the House will agree with me that
the place to which our merchants and manufacturers of eastern Canada
must look for enlarged markets is Manitoba and the North-west Territories; and there will be no markets there unless we have the population.
So far as I have been able to observe the Galicians — and I have taken the
trouble to drive out and go through the settlements, and even to go from
house to house, for the purpose of seeing them; and I have interviewed
many people of sound judgment who have taken the trouble to ascertain
the fact, who have gone out there to inquire and form a fair opinion
without prejudice and without desire to make political capital either for or
against the Government — as a whole, they are most desirable settlers. So
far as we have had them coming into the country up to the present time,
we have no cause to find fault. I do not say that it would be desirable to get
50,000 or 100,000 of these people in one year. I do not think it would. But
I do say we can well assimilate five or six thousand of them every year for
the next twenty years. And there would be no danger to the institutions of
Canada from the fact that, at the end of ten years, we may have fifty thousand Galicians in the North-west. Our experience of these people teaches
us that they are industrious, careful and law-abiding, and their strongest
desire is to assimilate with Canadians. Dr. Robertson, the general
superintendent of the Presbyterian Church in Manitoba and the North-
west Territories, has spoken in the highest terms of these people and has
expressed the warmest commendation of the policy the Government has
followed in bringing them in. He entertains the same opinion that I do,
that it would be proper for us to encourage them to come and to make

agriculturists of them and it would be no menace to the future of the country, but, on the contrary, they will assist in the developing of the country and become good citizens. So far as their general habits are concerned, I may say that we as members of the House of Commons are prepared to say that we would not allow people to come into Canada because they have been unfortunate enough to live in poverty in the countries from which they come. I venture to say that the ancestors of many prominent citizens of Canada were poor in the country whence they came, and nobody thinks less of them on that account. They are people, as my hon. friend said, of good physique, and they are people of good intellectual capacity; and they are moral and well-living people. I desire to call special attention to that — to their moral habits of life. I venture to say there is no part of the population of Canada — and I am not seeking to disparage my own countrymen for the sake of making an argument — more law-abiding or more moral in their habits, one with the other, than the Galicians.

[........]

don't let poverty stop them from coming (handwritten)

SOURCE: *House of Commons Debates,*
July 7, 1899, 6828-6868

No. 2: Commons Debates, April 12, 1901, Concerning Ukrainian Immigration

SUPPLY IMMIGRATION

MR. OLIVER: [........] I am here to say to-night that I believe the present conditions of the country would be better, our prosperity would be greater, we would have a still larger number of good settlers, if we did not have that class of immigration at all.

The idea was conveyed to the hon. members of this House that these people are occupying country that no other people will occupy. Speaking of the part of the country from which I come, and which I represent, I know more of this subject than any other hon. member of this House, bar none. The people are occupying land that is good for any people. They are occupying land that, if they were not occupying it, would be occupied by other people, either now or in the very near future, and the fact that they are occupying this land is a deterent to other people from occupying not only that land, but the land in their neighbourhood. Let me tell this House that, when the American settler makes inquiry as to settlement in this country, the first inquiry he makes is: What is the class of people in the locality in which he desires to settle, and I can tell you that the greatest objection that can be raised is that that part of the country has the presence of

Am. settlers (handwritten)

the very class of people which the hon. member for Selkirk (Mr. Mc-Creary) lauded so highly this afternoon.

I am not questioning the motives of any hon. member of this House. I am not questioning any motives in respect to the policy of the government at all, but I am here to state what I know for the information of the House and of the country. It is very well for us to theorize, and to say what might, could or should be, but it is desirable that we should, in discussing this and kindred questions, come down to facts, and understand whether we are doing the very best that can be done in the circumstances or not. We all want to see the western country settle up, and it is merely a question of what is the best policy to be pursued in order to settle that country up. If it can be shown that the inducement or acceptance of a certain class of immigrants is detrimental to the best interests of that country, and to the settlement of that country, then, I say, it is time to prevent, instead of encouraging, that class of settlement. I speak strongly on this point, because I find that there is a tendency on the part of people of this part of the country, not only in parliament but out of parliament, to suppose that the prosperity, welfare and progress of that country depends upon the continuation of this tide of immigration of the character of which the hon. member for Selkirk speaks. It is so far wide of the mark that I would be altogether falling in my duty as a member of this House and as a representative of that country, if I did not call attention, in the strongest language, to the facts of the case. What that country is to-day, it is because of the exertions, the sacrifices and the abilities of the men of eastern Canada, who have spread themselves over those plains and through those mountains, who are developing the industries and resources of that country, and who are building up a nation, a Canada, such as you have here, and, we hope, better than you have here. I say they cannot do that to advantage if their efforts are handicapped by the presence in thousands and tens of thousands of a class of people who, however worthy they may be, however capable they may be as agriculturists, are not and cannot be citizens of this country, as we would wish them to be citizens, to take part with us in the building up of a civilization and a social system there which are a necessary part of success in the settlement of any country. It is not enough to produce wheat out of the ground. We do not live to produce wheat. We live to produce people, to produce a social condition, and to build up a country, and if you give us only those who can produce wheat, and who cannot take their places as citizens, you do us an injury, and you place an obstacle in the way of our progress, instead of conferring an advantage upon us.

I have heard hon. members say that these strange people, these Slavs, will assimilate with the other people. Do you know what that word "assimilate" means? It is a nice sounding word. Do you know that it means

that if you settle on a farm on the prairies amongst them or in their
neighbourhood you must depend for the schooling of your children on the
tax-paying willingness and power of people who neither know nor care
anything about schools? Do you know that it means the intermarriage of
your sons or daughters with those who are of an alien race and of alien
ideas? That is assimilation, or else there is no assimilation. There is no
assimilation, and there will be no assimilation for many, many years, and
the whole country will suffer a drawback to that extent for a number of
years.

[........]

Let me say one word to the government, and it will be a word of advice. I speak here to-night on behalf of the most populous constituency in
the west; and I have reason to believe that I speak the sentiments of the
majority of the people between Lake Superior and the Rocky Mountains
on this immigration question. There is no question that the people of the
west feel more strongly on than this immigration question, and there is
nothing that they more earnestly resent than the idea of settling up the
country with people who will be a drag on our civilization and progress.
We did not go out to that country simply to produce wheat. We went to
build up a nation, a civilization, a social system that we could enjoy, be
proud of, and transmit to our children; and we resent the idea of having
the millstone of this Slav population hung around our necks in our efforts
to build up, beautify and improve that country, and so improve the whole
of Canada. I say it is an unpopular policy in western Canada to encourage
this Slav immigration. That may be a low ground on which to put the
question; but it is a business ground, and business is business. It may be a
low ground, and yet it is a high ground; because who are to be the judges
as to what is best for the interests of the North-west except the people who
have built it so far, and upon whom must rest the chief burden of building
it up to the height of prosperity to which we all expect it to attain.

MR. D. C. FRASER: [........] We cannot put on too fine airs about
our surroundings. Any man must wish sometimes that he could avoid
meeting this man, that man or the other. But we must not be too particular — least of all a politician who, in the course of an ordinary campaign, must meet people whom he had rather not meet on other occasions.
But I am willing to let any honest man come into Canada, any man who
will till the soil or work for a wage and give a fair return in labour for that
wage. I call upon the civilization of our country as represented by the
government and upon the higher civilization of our country as represented
by our societies and churches, to join in lifting these men up and making
them good citizens of our great west. For, if we wait for population to go
from the east to the west, that land will remain sterile and unproductive
for centuries to come. We have six millions of people in Canada — and

terror in the hearts of some of them because 7,000 Galicians have come amongst us. Dr. Robertson, of the Presbyterian Missions, relates an incident that shows what we may expect of these people. It may be a small matter, but to my mind it indicates that these Galicians will make that country a better country than it is. He was passing a school, a school that was taught by an English teacher, while the children were just beginning to learn English. He saw a little girl with blue eyes and fair hair —

Some hon. MEMBERS. Oh, oh.

Mr. FRASER: Oh, hon. gentlemen opposite need not interpose. I will relieve their feelings by saying that she was not more than that high. Dr. Robertson said to the little girl: 'You are a Galician, are you?' 'No, sir', said she, 'I am a Canadian.' This is one of the things to indicate what has happened in the history of every nation in the world among whom outside people have come to live — the newcomers have caught the spirit of the country and their surroundings and have become good citizens. And particularly does this happen when the newcomers come out into liberty from barbarism and oppression. There is no better way to make good citizens than to remove people from despotism and give them liberty to expand their energies. I am not afraid of these people. And why? Because I am not afraid of myself. If I lived in the North-west, I would not be afraid of 17,000 Galicians, I would feel humiliated if I could not take my place against ten or twenty or fifty people that could not speak my language. I hope the Dominion of Canada will be broad in this matter. I would exclude any vicious man from Canada if I could. I would put a mark on any criminal seeking to come in. But I should be ashamed of myself if I desired to keep out of Canada any man who came here to better his condition and who was willing to toil at any legitimate employment for a wage that would support himself and family. I admit that I do not know as much about that country as my hon. friend from Alberta. But the hon. gentleman is not the only one who is entitled to express an opinion on this matter. [........]

SOURCE: *House of Commons Debates*,
April 12, 1901, 2927 - 2978

In 1907, the idea of creating a distinct Ukrainian affiliate of the Socialist Party of Canada was raised, principally to facilitate political work among radicalized Ukrainian workers. The issue of autonomy as outlined in the initial draft of the statutes for the proposed Ukrainian Socialist Alliance reflected the concern among the proponents about maintaining the Ukrainian character of the organization. Significantly, in later years, the question of autonomy became a crucial issue which would force Ukrainian-Canadian socialists to break away from the Socialist Party of Canada.

No. 3: *Draft of Statutes for the Ukrainian Socialist Alliance, Socialist Party of Canada, 1907*

DRAFT OF STATUTES
Ukrainian Socialist Alliance — Socialist Party of Canada
(Produced by the Ukrainian Winnipeg Branch of the SPC)

In the province of Manitoba, Saskatchewan, Alberta and British Columbia there are over one hundred thousand Ukrainian proletarians whose ignorance of the English language and narrow cultural standard allow them to be exploited by Canadian capitalists. Only organization and education will liberate and elevate these most oppressed masses and place them in the ranks of the international army fighting for socialism. This work among the Ukrainian masses can be accomplished most effectively and quickly in their own language. This need suggests the formation of the Ukrainian Socialist Alliance — Socialist Party of Canada.

1. The U[krainian] S[ocialist] A[lliance] accepts the programmes of the SPC and is a constituent part of that body.
2. The Ukrainian Socialist Alliance — SPC has as its objective the organization of proletarians who speak Ukrainian.
3. The Ukrainian Socialist Alliance is comprised of "Independent Committees" which in their general meeting will select a committee of the Alliance that will carry out in turn the will of the body.

4. In the matter of organization, agitation, propaganda and publication, the Ukrainian Socialist Alliance has full autonomy.

[........]

SOURCE: *Червоний Прапор*,
(Red Banner), No. 1, November 15, 1907
[Translated from Ukrainian]

Established in 1910 through the efforts of a professional intelligentsia, the **Ukrainian Voice** *became a factor in the formative experience of Ukrainian ethnic consciousness in Canada. Espousing a liberal credo, the paper stressed the need for group solidarity, cultural awareness and education in order for Ukrainian Canadians to successfully compete in the economic marketplace. The emphasis on group consciousness naturally led the paper to support the national movement in the Ukrainian homeland.*

No. 4: Editorial, Our Road, **Український Голос (Ukrainian Voice),** *No. 1, March 16, 1910*

OUR ROAD

[........]

In large measure, the character of this country and especially in its western parts, is agrarian; therefore an opportunity exists for our people — historically suited to agriculture — to create for themselves a good existence, but only if they are able to obtain the same rights as the indigenous population. Theoretically, even though rights exist for everyone, until this time we have been discriminated against every step of the way. We know that our people occupied the worst land and in part this happened because our people were ignorant, poor and they did not know how to prevent this; but it is also the fault of those advisors (of ours), whom the government pays, because they mercilessly preyed upon our people.

Moreover, that portion of our immigrants who remain journeymen are the least paid and the most exploited of all the workers of other nationalities.

This then is the overall view of economic relations in which one finds, today, our people in Canada.

In relation to the political situation, even though all people here have equal rights, we did not make any progress because of our political naiveté. True, here, we have the general, equal and direct right to vote, but political swindlers, taking advantage of our people's ignorance, haggle over us even worst than they would over animals. In short, [there exists] total political demoralization, especially amongst our own people. But having this right, as well the right of freedom of speech, freedom of religion, free access to education, we, through energetic work, will be able to pave a road and arrange a life for ourselves according to our own wishes.

Therefore, in order to trace the life of our people with all of its economic, political and general cultural deficiencies and faults, as well as [further] prevent these deficiencies, we are publishing the *Ukrainian Voice*.

Ukrainian Voice sets for itself the task of defending at every opportunity the interests of the Ukrainian people, to educate them in every way, to assist in raising their economic and cultural level in order for them to stand on par with the other peoples of Canada.

SOURCE: *Український Голос*
(*Ukrainian Voice*), No.1, March 16, 1910
[Translated from Ukrainian]

Concerned with the 'enormous human wastage', Bishop Budka appealed for government intervention to assist Ukrainians in overcoming the initial hardships of homesteading. Budka was equally disturbed by growing social tensions which arose from nativist hostility associated with the onset of war and the migration of Ukrainian agriculturists from the rural areas to the urban centres. By 1914, an increasing number of Ukrainians were abandoning the homesteads in search of available work and relief in the cities.

No. 5: Memorandum from Bishop N. Budka on the Status and Improvement of the Ruthenians of Canada, January 31, 1914

MEMORANDUM
On the Status & Improvement of the Ruthenians of Canada

There are at present over 245,000 Ruthenians living in Canada. They live scattered over the whole area of the Dominion, but by far the greatest portion of them — nearly 75% — inhabit the western agricultural Provinces — Manitoba, Saskatchewan and Alberta. Taken as a whole, this nearly quarter of a million Ruthenians present a most peculiar aspect, — both from the economical and the social point of view respectively. Having had to leave their native country, owing to various forms of oppression, they have found at last political freedom but at the same time they find themselves handicapped by another chain of unfavorable social and economic conditions.

Ruthenian immigrants come to Canada from two unfortunate countries, where for political reasons, governments choose to keep them down by paralyzing popular education.

Anxious to preserve their own ancient civilization, their language, art, religion, democratic customs and independent spirit, the Ruthenians emigrate to Canada conscious of enormous difficulties. They come regardless of perils of sea, of distance, severe climate and rough country. They know very well, that hard work awaits them here and once in Canada they do, and are doing now, their fair share of work building docks, railways and cities. Through undaunted perseverance they succeed often, where others fail. Still, surrounded by classes which come from independent and well-managed countries, where education is considered the chief asset of civilization, the Ruthenian colonists, ignorant of the language and customs of this country and being in addition either farmers or unskilled laborers, are evidently at a tremendous disadvantage. Moreover, they come from countries of entirely different agricultural and industrial methods. In consequence of this, they very seldom can avail themselves of the various economical opportunities. As result, one part leads only an existence of bare vegetation while another part, which earns more, with a great struggle — instead of investing the surplus in some Canadian industries, sends ready money abroad, depriving thus both, themselves and Canadian trade, of working capital. In this way both classes — the destitute and the earning one — suffer enormously, and living as practical strangers in this country, fail to do justice not only to themselves but to their adopted country as well.

The educational dept. of the Ruthenian Mission in Canada is trying to remedy this serious evil by lectures, popular newspapers, schools and meetings, but cannot help seeing clearly, that in view of the truly gigantic task, these efforts are entirely inadequate.

Nothing but the Canadian government's energetic action can do something adequate, to improve the truly precarious condition of the Ruthenians.

We fully appreciate the efficiency of the Canadian Immigration Board and admire the results obtained by advertisements of Canada's advantages. All the same we do not think that colonizing efforts should cease when immigrants, Canada's flesh and bones, are passed by the Health authorities. It should be borne in mind, that not every class of colonist is fully capable of taking care of itself, once it has been handed over to some enterprising agency. On the contrary, from very close observation of the colonists' life we claim to be justified in asserting, that the proper colonizing system should be applied to colonists after their arrival in Canada and certain methods should be observed to turn these colonists into useful citizens, without taking present risks and tolerating enormous wastage of human material.

By way of an illustration only, we may mention, that much more up to date and more scientific methods are employed to import and adapt to the soil useful hardy plants and domestic animals, than in classifying and utilizing the most precious element of civilization: the colonist. No attempt nor pretence even is being made to understand or study the special character or abilities of immigrants. If not a cripple, the new arrival is from the steamer into the waiting train and dumped wholesale at the other end of the railway, wherever there seems to be an empty place in the country. Let him grow there at his own risk and expense. Absolutely no one will give himself any bother to inquire, how he does succeed; and if not, why not.

Of course the ignorance of the language not only handicaps the immigrant at the outset. It places him in the most unenviable position for ever afterwards. Only very few lucky ones have, later on, some chance of acquiring a knowledge of English. The overwhelming majority of the Ruthenian population is living in the country as total strangers. Neither the Ruthenians know how to avail themselves of various resources and opportunities in Canada nor do the Government know how to educate them, how to organize and assist them. The result is simply this, that thousands of disappointed and brokenhearted Ruthenians leave this country every year, although under certain circumstances they could have developed into most desirable and productive citizens. Also, very considerable amounts of money, some hundreds of thousands, earned by Ruthenians, is being sent every year abroad, because absolutely no effort is being made to retain this capital in Canada. This state of affairs is very unsatisfactory and similar waste of wealth should not be any longer tolerated.

An office of *General Commissioner for the Canadian Ruthenians, as a permanent organ of mutual communication between the Government and the Ruthenians should be established* without delay.

Through this office statistical data concerning the Ruthenian population, its needs and condition, should be collected, checked and compared. With an exact and unbiassed knowledge of Ruthenian affairs thus obtained, some means of remedying the existing evils could be found and carried out, for the lasting benefit of the country.

Simultaneously we are bound to draw Government's attention to the fact, that in the interest of mutual understanding between the English and Ruthenian people a permanent *Lecturer on Ruthenian history, literature and art,* at one of Canada's Western Universities should be appointed.

We know by bitter experience that Ruthenians are very far from being rightly understood in Canada. Some very serious misunderstandings and prejudices as to the Ruthenian race and its aspirations are widely spread amongst the English people, owing to the total ignorance of Ruthenian history, literature and art. At least the younger generation should have an opportunity of learning something definite and conclusive about their Ruthenian neighbors. We firmly believe, that this will prove an excellent instrument for establishing closer and more friendly relations between these two races and will contribute towards Canada's intellectual supremacy.

Winnipeg, Man., January 31st. A.D. 1914

> [sgd.] NICETAS BUDKA
> Ruthenian Catholic Bishop
> for the Ruthenian Mission of Canada

SOURCE: Hoover Institution Archives,
Petrushevich Collection, Box No. 3,
File: Commissioner in Canada

*The outbreak of hostilities between Austria-Hungary and
Tsarist Russia prompted the Ukrainian Greek Catholic Bishop
N. Budka to urge Ukrainians in Canada to return and defend
their homeland in eastern Galicia. His advocacy of the position
that even those Ukrainians who had decided to settle permanently
in Canada take up arms on the Austro-Hungarian side can only
be understood in the context of the limited war foreseen in July
1914. With the outset of world war Budka's originally emotive
appeal was tempered by the realization that the Canadian state
obliged Ukrainian Canadians as citizens to lend their une-
quivocal support to the war aims of the British Empire.*

No. 6: Pastoral Letter of Bishop N. Budka, July 27, 1914, Call-ing on Ukrainians to Return to Austria-Hungary and Assist Austria in the European Conflict

**TO THE REVEREND CLERGY AND ALL THE FAITHFUL OF
CANADIAN RUS'-UKRAINE**

For a number of years great misfortune has befallen our old
Fatherland. It is not only misery which has driven thousands of our
brothers into the wide world — the consequence of flooding which has
turned into wide-spread famine — but also moral indignation, in particular, the demoralization of our brethren in Galicia and in Hungary
through the mass of spies, agents, brochures and newspapers paid for by
the rubles of our neighbour — Russia, whether directly through Russia or
[indirectly] through Serbia, America and Canada.

Looming over this unfortunate state of affairs for a number of years
now has been the spectre of war, which the peace-loving Franz Josef I has
always tried to avert and postpone.

Then an incident occured which would try the patience of even the
most tolerant of men. On June 28 of this year the Austrian heir to the
throne, Franz Ferdinand — a man of great hope at this difficult moment
for Austria — died, along with his wife, from the bullet of a Serbian student. The loss of an experienced heir to the throne was painful to the old

monarch, Franz Josef, as well as to all the peoples of Austria and especially we Ruthenians, who placed in him great and justifiable hopes. The
enemies of Austria, especially the enemies of Ruthenian-Ukrainians, do
not disguise their joy in the wake of this tragedy.

Canadian Ruthenian-Ukrainians sympathizing with the misfortune
of our old Fatherland, expressed their feelings in church services for the
slain, and through prayers for the fate of their dear country.

Today, misfortune is at its height because there can be added to [this]
misery the greatest misfortune of all — war — which for the time being is
with Serbia but, probably, in a short while, with Russia as well — a war
which today has inestimable consequences that could not only change the
character of Austria but all of Europe as well and which most especially
could affect Ruthenians.

The old Emperor of Austria has not lived to enjoy a peaceful death;
his reign began with war in 1848 and at the end of his long life the Most
High has not been spared that cross and misfortune from which he tried
for such a long time to protect his subjects; now he must wage war.

An official appeal has reached Canada calling upon Austrian subjects, who are under military obligation, to return to Austria and prepare
to defend the country.

God only knows what will happen. Perhaps we will have to defend
Galicia from seizure by Russia with its appetite for Ruthenians; maybe we
will have to defend our parents, wives, children, brothers and our entire
land before the insatiable enemy. Perhaps after the war we will remain in
an unchanged Austria or [a country] strengthened by millions of our
brothers from abroad, but it is also possible that we will find ourselves
under the heavy hand of the Muscovite despot. All of this, which is in the
hands of God, we cannot predict. In any event, all Austrian subjects
should be at home in a position ready to defend our native land, our dear
brothers and sisters, our nation. Whoever is called upon should go to defend the threatened Fatherland. Those who have not been summoned and
are unregistered but are subject to military service — as well as deserters
— have been granted amnesty by the Emperor, that is to say a pardon
from punishment, only if they appear at the consulate and return to the
old country in defence of the Fatherland.

For those who have decided to remain for the rest of their lives in the
new Fatherland, Canada, but are bound to the old country through part of
their lives, should also participate in this great adventure of Austria's and
of our native brothers': for indeed, it is there that the fate of our people is
being decided.

Our participation should not be restricted only to reading newspapers in order to find out about the developments of war but we should help our old Fatherland as much as possible.

[........]

NIKITA, BISHOP

Winnipeg, Man., 27 July, 1914

This letter is to be read in all churches.

SOURCE: *Канадійський Русин* *(Canadian Ruthenian)*, August 1, 1914 [Translated from Ukrainian]

No. 7: Pastoral Letter of Bishop N. Budka, August 6, 1914, Retracting Pastoral Letter of July 27

TO THE REVEREND CLERGY AND THE FAITHFUL CANADIAN RUTHENIAN-UKRAINIANS

Not long ago, the news that Austria was at war with Serbia shocked the whole world. All other states adopted a patient attitude, and England especially strove with all its might to localize the war and restore peace.

At the time when no state was at war—with the exception of Austria and Serbia—and England did not summon its subjects in defence of their homeland, we published a pastoral letter in which we indicated that Austria, through the I[mperial] Consulate in Canada, was calling its subjects to rally around the Austrian flag; we said that those Ruthenians who had come to Canada for a short while should obey Austria's call and defend their families and property. But now, in the course of a few days, political relations have changed completely. Today, war has engulfed all of Europe; today, England as well as all of the British state are threatened by enemies; today, our new homeland, Canada, calls on its faithful subjects to rally around the English flag ready to give up their property and lives for the good of the British state.

Today, all nations who live under the flag of the British state send their sons to defend it.

So at this time when England turns to us as its faithful subjects with the call that we stand under its flag — when the British state requires our assistance — as loyal sons of the British state, we Canadian Ukrainians have a great and holy duty to stand under the flag of our new homeland, under the flag of the British state, and sacrifice, if necessary, our property and our blood.

Ruthenians! Citizens of Canada! It is our great duty to stand in defence of Canada because this country — which embraced us — and where we found not only bread but the possibility of spiritual growth — provides protection under the banner of liberty of the British Empire.

It is our holy duty to be prepared to sacrifice our property and blood for the good of Canada because it is to our new homeland that we swore loyalty and duty to give up all of our property and lives if ever this would be required of us.

This is our treasured homeland because here are our families, our children, all of our property, our heart, and our entire future.

Therefore, in this difficult moment, we must remember that as loyal sons of Canada, faithful to the oath [sworn] to the [new] homeland and our king, we must rally around the flag of the British state.

Set aside all party differences and misunderstanding; set aside all indifference and insouciance.

Conscious of our feeling of deep attachment and obligation, we want and will help our new homeland when it is threatened by our enemy.

Ruthenians, citizens of Canada! You who have already sworn an eternal oath to our king, George V, as well as those of you who are not yet citizens but wish to become so, remember that the oath obligates you to loyalty. For any act or word of disloyalty, in our country as well as others in a state of war, there awaits the penalty of death for traitors. Loyalty requires actions as well as sacrifices, and if the country calls and needs as such, [then] everyone must be prepared to sacrifice his life. If it were necessary to form Ruthenian regiments out of Canadian-Ruthenian citizens, then this would surely show that Ruthenians in Canada are true citizens prepared to sacrifice everything, even their lives, for their homeland. But again we would like to indicate that we must fulfill this obligation not only out of compliance with the laws but also with profound regard for our obligations.

God alone knows how this greatest war in history will end. Let us fervently pray to God that He deign, through His almighty power, to bring this war to a speedy conclusion and that our new Fatherland, Canada, should suffer no harm.

In view of our previous letter of 27 July which referred to that moment when the war was exclusively between Austria and Serbia and few believed that war would spread to other states; and in view of the neutral position of England which did not summon its subjects to defend their own state, we emphatically declare, that our previous letter of 27 July of this year no longer applies under the changed political situation and must not be read publicly in the churches. Instead, we order all priests to read this, our pastoral letter, during Divine Services in their parishes and instruct

Ruthenians, in accordance with this letter, about our obligations to the British state.

Given in Winnipeg, 6 August 1914
NIKITA, BISHOP

SOURCE: *Канадійський Русин*
(Canadian Ruthenian), August 8, 1914
[Translated from Ukrainian]

Social, economic and political differentiation created divisions within the Ukrainian-Canadian community. The formation of the Ukrainian Greek Orthodox Church of Canada in 1918 was prompted by dissatisfaction with a Catholic hierarchy which had tried to reassert its control over Ukrainian-Canadian life. Around this new church a secular leadership that was overtly Ukrainian would coalesce.

No. 8: Letter from the National Committee Calling on Delegates to a Conference for the Purpose of Forming a National Church, May 27, 1918

CONFIDENTIAL

Saskatoon, Sask., May 27th, 1918

Honoured Sir!

You are probably aware that our [Ukrainian] religious-national affairs have become very disquieting at this time. Notwithstanding the fact that our Greek Catholic Church — to which the majority of our people in Canada belong — was able to obtain (after much petitioning) the services of a bishop in the person of His Most Reverend Nikita Budka, the Greek Catholic faithful still do not have adequate spiritual counsel: first, there are too few Greek Catholic priests; and second, of those few priests, not all are given to serve their high calling. Moreover, these priests are celibates and are not married, which our religious rite and our religious-national tradition requires. Most annoying of all, however, is the fact that the operation of our Greek Catholic Church is conducted according to the wishes and under the strict control of the French Roman Catholic Church, often in opposition to our national interest.

You are also undoubtedly aware, Sir, that in the last while a fight has developed between the clergy under Bishop N. Budka and the intelligentsia which congregates around such national institutions as the educational, and reading halls, where the clergy wishes to strengthen clerical control over [these] national institutions and in general over all of the national work. It has even come to the point where His Most Reverend in conjunction with the clergy have resorted to using medieval measures against their detractors, for example, refusing to confess the Greek Catholic faithful who are members of national institutions, denying them burial in church cemeteries, and even threatening the leaders of national institutions and all of the people organized in these institutions with excommunication.

We believe that our religious-national affairs are in a very distressing and discomforting situation and it is necessary now, without further delay, to prevent it from further deteriorating. We were forced to discuss this matter with many knowledgeable people and they urge us to take quick action. Consequently, we are planning to call in Saskatoon, within six weeks time, a confidential meeting of enlightened individuals who have some influence with the people. This gathering will present to His Most Reverend Bishop Budka — especially invited to the meeting — our requests in the matter of religious-national work, requests which have the aim of dismissing the accusations made against our national religious organizations.

This confidential meeting will be called by a committee of some thirty individuals, to whose ranks we have the honour of inviting you as well. We believe that you will not turn down our request, recognizing the historical importance of the work that this committee hopes to undertake.

Please inform us of your decision by return mail at the following address:

National Committee 716 Lasdown Ave. Saskatoon, Saskatchewan

Sincere regards,

FOR THE COMMITTEE

[sgd.] V. SWYSTUN

[————]

P.S. Saskatoon has been chosen as the site of the meeting because of its central location in Western Canada.

Please discuss this matter with Messrs. Arsenych and Ferley.

SOURCE: Hoover Institution Archives,
Petrushevich Collection, Box No. 3,
File: Commissioner in Canada
[Translated from Ukrainian]

---

*No. 9: Resolutions of National Church Conference, July 1918,
Establishing the Ukrainian Greek Orthodox Church of Canada*

National Church Meeting, July 18-19, 1918

RESOLUTIONS

[Resolution I]

WHEREAS, the head of the Ruthenian Greek Catholic Church unconditionally demands that full title to communal church property be given to the Ruthenian bishopric corporation, which in accordance with its regulations comprise the bishop, Ruthenian Greek Catholic parishes or missions of which the only administrator and representative is the bishop, and

WHEREAS, in accordance with the regulations of this corporation, Ruthenian Greek Catholic parishes are deprived of all rights to manage their communal church property, and

WHEREAS, the aforementioned bishop refused to admit the spiritual jurisdiction of married Ukrainian priests in Canada (which is contrary to the rights and privileges of our faith) and in fact introduced celibates, and

WHEREAS, the aforementioned bishop grants Roman Catholic missionaries, Redemptorist priests, jurisdiction among our Ruthenian Greek Catholic people, and

WHEREAS, this bishop accords himself exclusive right and control over all our education and other institutions as well as our aspirations, and

WHEREAS, this aforementioned bishop administers church affairs against all democratic principles of this country which are upheld by the Ukrainian people, and

WHEREAS, the aforementioned bishop often conducted himself in a manner as to compromise Ukrainians in Canada, and

WHEREAS, all appeals, petitions and attempts by representative elements of the Ukrainian people, urging the bishop to fulfill his obligations with greater tolerance and procedure, were unsuccessful, and

WHEREAS, the aforementioned bishop, in a clearly un-Christian manner, refuses spiritual services to those parishes which did not want to relinquish their communal church property without some safeguards under the bishopric corporation, and

WHEREAS, the aforementioned bishop threatens excommunication against members of many educational organizations in Canada which are not under his control and further instructed his priests not to give confession or absolution to these members, and

WHEREAS, the present Ruthenian Greek Catholic Church is the result of a church union forced upon a portion of the Ukrainian nation by Poland in 1596 and which was supported by Austria.

Therefore, we the representatives of Ukrainian congregations and communities in Western Canada, resolve as follows:

To Establish a Ukrainian Greek Orthodox Church in Canada
on the following principles:

a) The church is in communion with other Eastern Orthodox Churches and accepts the same dogmas and the same rite.

b) The priests shall be married.

c) Communal church property shall belong and be managed by parishes.

d) All bishops shall be chosen by a general Sobor of priests and delegates from parishes and brotherhoods.

e) Parishes have the right to appoint or dismiss priests.

f) In order to fulfill the aims and objectives of this conference, it is resolved to organize the Ukrainian Greek Orthodox Brotherhood of Canada which shall

1) Incorporate the newly formed church in Canada

2) Establish a Ukrainian Greek Orthodox Seminary

3) Organize Ukrainian Greek Orthodox parishes

4) Obtain appropriate priests for each parish

5) Prepare for and call a Sobor composed of supporters and members of this church to complete its organization

[........]

Resolution III

Since Bishop Budka, head of the Greek Catholic church in Canada, wishes to appear as the representative of Ukrainians in Canada but with false political views and incivility brings grief to the Ukrainian people, and

Since a significant proportion of Ukrainian residents in Canada do not recognize Bishop Budka as such a representative and do not agree with his politics and tactics,

Therefore, the present conference declares that it does not agree with the politics of Bishop Budka, that, on the contrary, Bishop Budka does not represent the sentiments of the Ukrainian people, and that responsibility for his harmful actions rests with him alone and not the people.

SOURCE: *Український Голос*
(Ukrainian Voice), No. 32, August 7, 1918
[Translated from Ukrainian]

The War-Time Elections Bill, introduced in September of 1917, disenfranchised immigrants who had been identified as enemy aliens. This measure was one of a number of steps undertaken by the state, including internment, to deal with the perceived threat of the East Central European foreign element in Canada. Those who petitioned for the rescinding of the Act noted the deleterious effects of this piece of legislation on Canadian nation-building efforts.

No. 10: Letter from H. A. Mackie, M.P., to Prime Minister R. L. Borden, October 16, 1918, Asking that the War-Time Elections Act be Rescinded

EDMONTON, ALTA.
October 16, 1918

To Sir Robert Borden
Prime Minister of Canada
Ottawa, Ont.

Sir:

Recently representations were made to me by the local Ruthenian Association that the "War Time Elections" Act ought to be rescinded so as

to permit the Ukrainians in Canada to render non-combatant service.
[........]

I desire to treat this subject from two points: First, Canadian, and secondly, from the International point of view as far as British interests are involved. In Canada the foreigners are of Slav extraction. The Ukrainians are most numerous amongst them. There are about 350,000 Ukrainians from Austria and about 150,000 from Russia. The Slav here is Russian, Galician, Bokivenian, or Ukrainian. Those from Russia are called Russians. [........]

The Ukrainians who came to Canada from Austria were invited by the Canadian Government from 1895, and induced by agents who, no doubt, worked for the Canadian Government, to leave their country of oppression where they had to toil for landlords, and were promised if they came to Canada they would get free land, and liberate themselves and become free men. Even as late as 1912-13-14 the Canadian Government vigorously upheld this propaganda in Austria among the Ruthenians (now properly called Ukrainians.) The agents of the C.P.R. even flattered these people by carrying them in a steamship called "Ruthenian." The Austrian Government, seeing the success of the Canadian propaganda amongst the Ruthenians took action against the C.P.R. Company in 1913-14, just before the war, to stop young men of military age from leaving Austria so as not to weaken the Austrian military forces. Nevertheless, the Canadian immigration figures show that in the years just before the war, and even after the war started, there came to Canada thousands of Ruthenians from Austria, always invited by the Canadian Government to come to share our benefits. They were disillusioned soon after the war started. The military authorities here, and especially the local subalterns apparently did not pay any attention to the fact that these people were invited and treated them all without distinction, as Austrians and enemies. Canadian public opinion was not educated to make distinction and all foreigners were Austrians or Austro-Hungarians. This bias against these people grew daily more hostile. The Canadian authorities have done nothing to educate public opinion. Besides, by inducing Austrians to come here just before the war, when immediately thereafter it became impossible to get British citizenship, public opinion was inflamed to such degree that all foreigners were treated alike, and in a hostile manner, so that some were displaced from employment and replaced by British born fellow-workers, who have seen in them only an alien enemy.

The 150,000 Ukrainians who came to Canada from Russia have been considered as Russians, although they are of the same nationality, spoke and speak the same language as those who came from Austria, but concealed their true nationality so as not to be treated as enemies, called themselves Russians, and enjoyed all the privileges accorded to their British brothers.

At the beginning of the war, hundreds or thousands of Ukrainians from Russia enlisted with the Canadian Expeditionary Forces as Russians, and no doubt the Canadian military statistical bureau would today show that most of these so-called Russians came from districts which are now in the territory comprising the Ukrainian State. Canadian recruiting officers soon discovered that those so-called Russians were nothing other than of the same stock of Ukrainians. Because they were not allowed to enlist as Austrians, they used fictitious names and gave false places of their birth to show that they came from Russia, some even calling themselves "Smith" and other English names. To estimate the number of Ukrainians who have enlisted in this way with the Canadian Expeditionary Forces would be very hard, as they were enlisting in various battalions from the Atlantic to the Pacific coast, but it is safe to say that, to the approximate half million soldiers in Canada, if the figures of the War Office were available, it could be shown that these people, per population, gave a larger percentage of men to the war than certain races in Canada have, after having enjoyed the privileges of British citizenship for a period of a century or more.

It has been argued in some quarters that the Ruthenians could have volunteered as noncombatants in any event if they so desired; but if you will view the condition of things fairly it is not difficult to understand why a people considered as enemies, disfranchised, refused naturalization, even to get patents when all homestead duties had been performed (a refusal which in many instances prevented the settler from securing loans and progressing in an agricultural way), you will not wonder that they did not offer themselves lest they might be considered as spies, and lest they might be taking chances upon being court-martialled and disposed of summarily as they knew they might be if they were living under Austrian and German rule.

You will probably recall that a number of them were returned to Canada from Britain on account of their birth. If the shoe is placed on the other foot, the reason for absence of volunteers is easily understood.

The deduction I desire to make from the foregoing observations is this:-

Invited to Canada to get freedom, guaranteed British "fair play" and yet discovering, without having full knowledge of the facts, that they are considered as enemies, it is not difficult to predict that, after the war is over, the tyranny of Europe is wiped away, the Ukrainian state of 300 years ago, with probable additions from Austria is a fact, a large number of Ukrainians in this country will repatriate themselves. Canadian public opinion, created by the action of the Government since the war, has made for oppression. Although it is true that, in Canada, they retain a desire to help their brothers in Europe to full independence, and to build up a

Ukrainian State, they have no political aspirations in Canada except the desire to be allowed to enjoy the rights awarded to all British subjects.

It may be interjected by opponents that they seek to maintain their language in schools. In this connection it must be remembered that the old folks cannot be transformed any more than it has been possible to transform conquered races in Europe, when after centuries they still remain distinct as races. But it is also true that the growing generations speak the English language fairly well, and have acquired the habits and customs of Canadians.

There is a further reason for the Ruthenian and Ukrainian desire to maintain their language. It is a religious one. The Greek Catholics as well as the Greek Orthodox worship according to the Eastern rites. Apart from a few differences in dogma, and the fact that the Greek Catholics are united with Rome, that is, they recognize the Pope as the head of the Church without submitting to him, whilst the Greek Orthodox recognized at one time the Czar of Russia as the head of their Church, there is no difference in the ritual. They claim that abolition of the Ukrainian language is to endanger the continuance of worship according to Eastern rites, and would only lead their people to worship according to the Latin rites, to adopt the Latin language, and so far as the Greek Catholics are concerned, it would lead them to the Roman Church.

[........]

I regret to say that their disfranchisement, in my opinion, has a strong retrospective effect on the younger generations who were quickly assimilating for they viewed the attitude of the Canadian people not of foreign extraction with a great deal of disfavor, and have compared the propaganda of freedom and liberty under British rule with the restriction of such freedom, even after British citizenship granted. They account to themselves they did not ask for exemption from military service and were prepared for the most part to shoulder all the responsibilities of citizenship. (I am willing to admit that there is a small and insignificant percentage of the foreign population still adhering to socialistic doctrines as they were brought from Europe but such factions have been losing in importance as the younger generations have had the advantages of understanding their British citizenship. Besides Canadian soil is most unfertile in giving perennial root to such doctrines.)

From another point of view it is regrettable the Government was obliged to take the step it did, because the doctrines I have described have been encouraged by pointing out to the foreigners at large that the boasted freedom is mere sham and pretension.

You will pardon me for dwelling on this point at length, but the views which are generally held by Canadians of these people are views which I, myself, held at one time, but which I learnt to correct by the study of their history and by personal contact.

I labour another point of Canadian interest. I have already indicated that on account of religious belief the Ukrainian population in Canada is likely to be slow of assimilation. The Province of Quebec has been slow of assimilation, both by reason of religion and language. Is there not possibly an advantage in this slow process of assimilation? We of the western provinces realize more than anybody in the Dominion the rapid Americanization of our Canadians by reason of the rapid invasion of our fertile prairies. When we view the population of both countries divided by an imaginary line, one wonders how we have been kept distinct even unto this day. If Canada has remained as it is, it is due, in my opinion, to the fear of being incorporated into American territory and thereby losing the advantages granted us under the British Crown, and particularly would this be the case with the province of Quebec. There is the undeniable fact that two millions of people as against one hundred millions of people, there is bound to be a great influence exerted on the smaller population. The slow assimilation is a guarantee that our American neighbors shall not gain too fast a hold on our Canadian people. If, therefore, after this war, by reason of the treatment accorded to our foreign population, they should repatriate, one of the checks to Americanization of the West has been removed.

Let us now discuss for a moment the International question. Without knowing anything of what may take place in Europe at the end of war, the geography of Europe suggests certain inevitable consequences. Europe, by population, stands:-

1. Germany with a population of seventy millions.
2. Russia with a population of sixty millions.
3. Ukrainia, in confederation with Russia as an autonomous state with a population of forty millions.
4. France with a population of thirty-eight millions.
5. Italy with a population of about thirty-five millions.

and the other countries respectively with smaller populations.

So far as geographical division in Europe is concerned there is an East and a West. The state which will be of the greatest importance to Britain and her colonies, not only from the viewpoint of population, is the Ukrainian State to be, because it is adjoining Turkestan in Asia, and holds the key to the situation of the extreme East in Europe, and as a matter of fact, is situated in that position which has been represented in history as the "Gate of Eastern Nations."

[........]

I have been hearing a great deal of recent date about the League of Nations, and I am bound to say I hold a grave doubt of the practicability of such a society capable of lasting over an indefinite period of time [........]. If I am right in my ramblings, then what should be the attitude of the British people, which includes our own country, with a view of maintaining international integrity? For future ages, in my mind, we should take steps to secure the goodwill of that state which will hold the key to the European situation.

My arguments for restitution of rights suspended to British subjects may be far-fetched, but at all events, I feel it my duty to argue this case from the angles that strike me, rather than to keep silence.

I desire to apologize for the length of this letter, and the seeming presumption on my part to offer suggestions. In conclusion I wish to disabuse the minds of anybody that I am writing from personal interest. Recently a reporter of the "Associated Press" called upon me and attempted to rebuke me for the views I held, and suggested that they were dictated with an advantage to be gained in future political contests. So far as that is concerned I assume that the same political tricks could be played by me as by others in gerrymandering a constituency. So far as the past contest is concerned, having in mind the majority with which I have been elected, every Ruthenian in my constituency could have voted against me, and I would still have been elected. I am not writing from a personal interest in this matter, and I have no care as to whether I am elected again or not. Such considerations are trivial in the light of the issues involved. The Roman Empire is an outstanding example of mistakes. The British Empire is still in the ascendency. Will it remain depends upon the cooperation of men, and the interchange of ideas. If I have not been of assistance to you I trust I have not committed a wrong. May I suggest before closing that a propaganda carried on at the present time by the leading Ukrainians and clergy might assist in gaining the objects discussed, and in unifying races rather than dividing them?

Objection is taken that their noncombatant work would interfere with labor and their organizations. Noncombatant workers need not disturb economic conditions. The present equilibrium can be maintained, and the surplus value of earning, can be diverted to a fund for returned soldiers.

Believe me,
Sir,
Yours very sincerely,

[sgd.] H. A. MACKIE
[Member of Parliament
East Edmonton]

SOURCE: Public Archives of Canada,
RG 13 A2, Vol. 228,
File: 2438

With the Versailles postwar peace negotiations underway, the Ukrainian Canadian Citizens' League, an ad hoc representative body whose aim was 'to interest Canadians in the case of Ukrainian democracy', appealed for direct Canadian intervention on behalf of the newly created Ukrainian Democratic Republic. They presented a geopolitical argument, claiming European political stability would be enhanced with the creation of an independent Ukraine. More immediately, however, the existence of Ukrainian identity in Canada bound Ukrainian Canadians to the political objective of a consolidated Ukrainian state.

No. 11: Petition of Ukrainian Canadian Citizens' League to Prime Minister R. L. Borden, April 24, 1919, Requesting Canadian Diplomatic Recognition for the Ukrainian Democratic Republic

Premier R. L. Borden
Canadian Peace Delegation
Paris

On behalf of the Ukrainian Canadian citizens, the Ukrainian Canadian Citizen's League requests [the] following: That your Government give immediate recognition to the Ukrainian Republic as such; that you, as [a] representative at [the] Peace Conference, use your good offices in helping to settle the boundaries of [the] Ukrainian Republic on ethnographical principals; that the Allied Government strengthen the Ukrainian Republic by compelling Poles to withdraw their forces from Ukrainian territory in general and Eastern Galicia and Cholm in particular; that [the] Allies [........] immediately repatriate one hundred thousand [........] Ukrainian soldiers, war prisoners held by Italy, and facilitate transportation of this force into [the] ranks of General Petlura. They are very anxious to join him and fight for their united mother country under the command against [the] Bolsheviki. Ukrania will become [a] bulwark against [the] Moscovite extreme in the North and the German pressure for the East [........]. We urge that your immediate intervention is highly essential, as the future welfare of not only Ukrania, but [the] whole [of] Europe, depends on the immediate action in this respect of those who have the leadership at the Peace Conference.

The Ukrainian Canadian Citizens League

SOURCE: Public Archives of Canada,
Borden Papers, MG 26 H1(C), Vol. 162

Internment operations and repressive state laws including disenfranchisement, censorship and deportation aimed at the ethnic labourer were introduced during the war and maintained after its conclusion. These measures were symptomatic of rampant nativism, war hysteria, and, later, fear of revolution. In the aftermath of the bloody Winnipeg General Strike of May 1919, advocates of force urged the government to continue to use the means at its disposal to subdue once and for all the most radicalized of the labour force — Ukrainians, Russians and Poles.

No. 12: Letter from the Hon. Sir Hugh Macdonald, Police Magistrate, to the Hon. A. Meighen, Minister of Interior, July 3, 1919, Expressing Opinion on the Desirability of Expulsion and the Use of Force to Subdue the Ethnic Labour Element

Winnipeg, Canada
3rd July 1919

Hon. Arthur Meighen K. C.
Minister of the Interior
Ottawa, Ont.

My dear Mr. Meighen:

Allow me to congratulate you on the stand which both Sir Robert Borden and yourself have taken with regard to the reinstatement of the postal employees here, who struck on the 15th of May last and to assure you that you never did anything more likely to enure to the benefit of the Unionist Party and of Canada than when you showed that no body of men — however numerous — would be allowed to upset the whole business of the country by stopping His Majesty's mail and that any who attempted to do so would be forced to leave the public service. I am, of course, sorry for some individuals who have lost their places through being carried away by the spirit of unrest which prevails here at present, as it does pretty much throughout the civilized world, but I cannot but recognize that there was no other course open to the Government than the one they have adopted, unless they wished to advertise the fact that members of the Civil Service had only to shake the mailed fist to secure anything they chose to demand, no matter how unreasonable their demands might be.

I must also congratulate you on the way you are dealing with the men at the head of the movement intended to introduce Government framed on the Russian model into Canada [........].

I should like to impress upon you too, the desirability of getting rid of as many undesirable aliens as possible and I venture to do so, because, as Police Magistrate, I have seen to what a large extent Bolsheviki ideas are held by the Ruthenian, Russian and Polish people, whom we have in our midst and how large a section of the Russian and German Jews hold similar views. I have always held that, as Police Magistrate, I occupy a position half way between a Judge and the father of a family and consequently I frequently make a point of seeing in the Police Magistrate's office and talking to prisoners who have been convicted before me for breaches of the Criminal law, and as I attempt to be their "friend, counsellor and guide," I necessarily learn more of their opinions than does the ordinary citizen, and I am perfectly convinced that we have a very bad and dangerous element in the good City of Winnipeg and that it is advisable, indeed that it is absolutely necessary that an example should be made to show them that law and order must be maintained and that all attempts to interfere by revolutionary means with our form of government, whether Federal, Provincial or Municipal, will be sternly repressed. Coming as these men do from countries where such a thing as freedom is unknown, they do not understand generous treatment and consider it is only extended to them because the Government is afraid of them; indeed, fear is the only agency that can be successfully employed to keep them within the law and I have no doubt that if the Dominion Government persists in the course that it is now adopting the foreign element here will soon be as gentle and as easily controlled as a lot of sheep. When I speak of the foreign element, I allude only to men of the races I have above mentioned, as here we find those coming from other countries no harder to handle and keep in order than our own people.

I am sure you must be glad to see the end of the session in sight and I hope you will spend at least part of the interval between the end of this session and the beginning of the next in taking a holiday and building up your constitution. Good people are scarce and consequently you and I must take care of ourselves.

With kindest regards and best wishes, I remain,

Your sincerely,

[sgd.] HUGH J. MACDONALD

SOURCE: Public Archives of Canada,
Meichen Papers, Series I, MG 26 I, Vol. 5

Lacking a state with international legal status which could have supported their assertion to a distinct national identity, those immigrants from Ukrainian lands who settled in Canada found themselves being classified as nationals of other states, such as Poland, or by regional appelations like Galician and Bukovynian. This condition retarded Ukrainian community-building efforts within Canada but later became a focal point for political activism.

No. 13: Letter from W. H. Walker, Assistant Under-Secretary of State for External Affairs to the Governor General, June 15, 1922, Regarding the Proper Description of Naturalized Persons whose Origins are from Western Ukrainian Territories

FROM DEPT. OF EXTERNAL AFFAIRS TO G[OVERNOR]
GENERAL'S SECRETARY

Sir,

I have the honour to state that the question has been raised by the Department of the Secretary of State of Canada of the proper description of persons naturalized under the Naturalization Acts, 1914 and 1920, whose origin was derived from the Province of Galicia or the adjoining portions of Russia which are now alleged to be established as the Ukrainian Republic.

It is pointed out that with respect to the portions of Galicia which under the Treaty of Versailles and the Protocol were declared to form part of the Republic of Poland, there is no question, such persons, although of Austrian origin, being now citizens of Poland under the Treaty, and being so described. Difficulty arises, however, with respect to those from the eastern part of Galicia, which is now under Polish administration, pending a plebiscite in 1914. So far as can be ascertained, the Treaties make no reference to the nationality of persons of this area. Strictly, such persons should be described as Austrians, and, as under the amendment of the Naturalization Act of 1920, former alien enemies may not be naturalized until the expiration of ten years from the termination of the war, they are precluded from naturalization if deemed to be Austrian. The Department of the Secretary of State of Canada, however, has relaxed its technical ruling in favour of applicants who are reported by the police to be good and law-abiding citizens and worthy of naturalization, and in their certificates they are described as Poles. Many of these persons object to such description, maintaining that they are Ukrainian or Ruthenian, and that they should be so described. The Department does not give weight to this suggestion, as there is no official notification of the establishment of the Ukrainian Republic. Moreover, there does not appear to be any good ground for describing persons whose origin was derived from the eastern portion of Galicia as Ukrainians, because they are not of origin of the territory which is now stated to be the Ukrainian Republic. The same difficulty arises with respect to persons of origin of those parts of Russia now stated to form part of the Ukrainian Republic.

As similar difficulties may have been considered by the Home Department, I am to request that His Excellency may be humbly moved to bring the matter to the attention of the Secretary of State for the Colonies, with the request that any available information may be supplied as to the practice followed in the United Kingdom in such cases.

I have, etc.

[sgd.] W. H. WALKER
Assistant Under-Secretary
for External Affairs

Rooted in the tenets of Social Darwinism and infused with xenophobia political lobbying was carried out by a number of influential Canadians against the immigration of Ukrainians both before and after World War I.

No. 14: One Language, One Flag, Saskatoon Phoenix, April 28, 1924

ONE LANGUAGE, ONE FLAG, PLEA MADE BY THE BISHOP

Nation-building was the subject of an earnest and eloquent sermon by the Rt. Rev. Dr. G. Exton Lloyd, Bishop of Saskatchewan [........]

Must Be Anglo-Saxon

"Build thou the walls of Jerusalem" (Psalm 51: 18) was the text upon which his Lordship based his address.

"If the nation is to do its proper work in the world, if it is to exercise the influence for which God has given it the talents, then we must insist on being a homogeneous people with a unity of language and loyalty. We must be welded into a body, and that body must be Anglo-Saxon and elements which cannot assimilate ought not be admitted into this country in its formative period. Of the thousands that are being poured into this Western country at the present time, of all sorts, kinds and conditions, languages, characters and loyalties of every sort, and nothing has the government taken to explain to this mixture, before they let them come here, that English is our language and British is our loyalty [........]"

Crime to West

"Has a pledge been taken from them before they land that they are willing to conform to these things? Have they been let come or induced to come without such warning or obligation? If the latter is the case, then the government is committing a crime against the Western country today, and 20 years hence. [........]

Bound to React

The sword is not the only way to defend the flag, and remember this, those who defend the flag in this country must expect bullets though they may be made of abuse instead of lead. The whole teaching of the Gospel and the circumstances of our own times coincide with great force. The sin

which Christ so frequently denounces is the sin of doing nothing, to let
things go as they are going. To let a vast population go on increasing and
multiplying with no restraining, regenerating influences until it becomes
unmanageable — this neglect, this indifference, this indolence and want of
forethought is bound to react on this nation in the days to come with
frightful consequences. To neglect the moral condition of our more and
more mixed population is national suicide. It is not too late now, but it
may easily be too late ten years from now as things are going in this
Western land."

[.......]

SOURCE: *Saskatoon Phoenix,*
April 28, 1924

*In 1927, the Ukrainian Self-Reliance League was formed
largely through the efforts of an important segment of the growing
Ukrainian professional class. The organization identified with
the Ukrainian Greek Orthodox Church of Canada and espoused
a liberal democratic creed. Although committed to the idea of
Ukrainian independence, the USRL was primarily oriented
toward organizing the Ukrainian community in Canada in
order to advance the objective of the community's social and
economic integration into the Canadian mainstream. This
political position was severely criticized by the more militant
Ukrainian-Canadian nationalists who viewed this as a retreat
from the cause of national liberation.*

No. 15: Ukrainian Self-Reliance League Programme, December 1927

PROGRAMME OF THE UKRAINIAN SELF-RELIANCE LEAGUE

1. Political Affairs

a) **Relationship to Canada** — Considering Canada as the newly
   adopted homeland of Ukrainians, the USRL urges Ukrainians as
   citizens to fully participate in all matters concerning this country, tak-

ing advantage of their civil rights and privileges as well as fulfilling their civic obligations.

Not being in the narrow sense of the term a political party, the USRL allows its individual members the freedom to vote the party of their choosing in Canadian dominion, provincial and municipal elections, although it forsees the possibility that, in special circumstances, the organization's interests could require the support of one party over another.

b) **Relationship to Ukraine** — With respect to Ukraine, the USRL places the state above any party.

On the basis of the argument that the even development and welfare of the Ukrainian nation can only be secured within the boundaries of an independent and sovereign state, the USRL considers the highest ideal of the Ukrainian nation to be the realization of Ukrainian state independence within its ethnographic territories.

Because the immediate neighbours of Ukraine, in particular Muscovy and Poland, have demonstrated throughout history their intransigent hostility to the idea of Ukrainian statehood, the USRL excludes the possibility of any permanent union or federation between Ukraine and its neighbours.

Moreover, the USRL opposes the occupation of Ukrainian territory by Russia, Poland, Romania and Czechoslovakia and considers its holy duty to work toward the total liberation of Ukrainian territory from these occupiers.

Apart from this, the USRL condemns the incursion of the Russian Bolshevik Party into Ukraine and its attack against the Ukrainian nation, replacing an independent, sovereign republic with a Soviet surrogate which Muscovites directly control from Moscow or indirectly control through their proxies in Kharkiv.

The USRL's position on Ukrainian parties in Europe, those nations which have occupied Ukrainian lands, other nations, and, in general, national and political matters will depend on how that position conforms to both the ideal of an independent Ukrainian state and a true and independent political course.

2. Economic Affairs

On the basis of the argument that all social classes — emerging from a social division of labour — are necessary for both economic and human progress and that classes rise and vanish in relation to the specific needs of the social order: the USRL believes that the economic good and the progress of humanity will occur more likely through the harmonizing of class differences rather than through class struggle.

From this point of view, the USRL accepts the idea of solidarism, or the harmonizing of class differences.

Aside from this, the USRL urges Ukrainian Canadians to conduct their economic life in such a way that, along with the farming and working classes, they would assist in expanding and supporting that class which is associated with trade, industry and the independent professions.

3. Church Affairs

The USRL maintains a positive position in relation to the church and religion, regarding all manifestations of religious indeterminism as ruinous.

The USRL recognizes the importance of the church and its work; it supports that church which works for the welfare of the Ukrainian people, is under its control and does not serve as an instrument for alien objectives.

SOURCE: *Союз Українців Самостійників в Канаді.* (Winnipeg: USRL, 1928)
[Translated from Ukrainian]

The prospect of war with its consequent loyalty implications further divided the Ukrainian community in Canada. The newly formed Ukrainian Self-Reliance League, through the editorials of **Ukrainian Voice,** *spoke unequivocally that Ukrainian support for Britain and the Dominions in the eventuality of war could never be in doubt. The belief stemmed from its own committment to building Ukrainian life in Canada as well the view that allegiance to liberal political democratic values would favour Ukrainian independence. It condemned the more militant nationalist element in the community whose demands, they felt, placed the issue of Ukrainian-Canadian allegiance in question and threatened the social gains made by Ukrainians thus far.*

No. 16: Editorial, Canadian Ukrainians and War, **Український Голос**
(Ukrainian Voice), *No. 40, October 3, 1928*

CANADIAN UKRAINIANS AND WAR

[........] from time to time there arrive in Canada individuals who are confused as a result of great pretensions. In their heads roars the sound of war, intervention and other similar phenomena associated with "high politics"; and having nothing better to do because they know nothing more, they swindle people out of their money and frighten them with the talk of a new war [........]. It is these people who raised the question: What would we do if war was to come about and if Great Britain participated in this war?

From our point of view, there cannot be two answers to this question. If Great Britain were to go to war and if Canada as a constituent member of the British Commonwealth were to join in the struggle, then Canadian Ukrainians should and could only do one thing as loyal Canadian citizens: together with other Canadian citizens they should assist Canada and Great Britain to win the war.

By creating an enemy camp against the country in which they live and of which they are citizens, Canadian Ukrainians will not benefit except for filling internment camps and prisons and encouraging all types of surveillance against their loved ones who did not even involve themselves. They experienced this lesson in the previous war. At that same time in Canada, when Ukrainians filled the internment camps, Haller formed his legions which were used to conquer Western Ukraine [........].

Canadian Ukrainians should be loyal to their country without regard as to whom Great Britain is allied or opposed to. Through their loyalty they will always be able to give greater assistance to the Ukrainian cause than through disloyalty, opposition and treason. The issue of loyalty for Canadian Ukrainians is made easier somewhat by the fact that it is impossible for Great Britain to be at war with Ukraine since an independent Ukrainian state does not exist; but if Great Britain was to oppose any one of those countries which currently occupy Ukrainian territories, then it would fight against an enemy of Ukraine. This is the reason why Ukrainians, not only in Canada but in Ukraine as well, have a common interest with Great Britain.

SOURCE: *Український Голос*
(Ukrainian Voice), No. 40, October 3, 1928
[Translated from Ukrainian]

*The Ukrainian Labour and Farmer Temple Association
(ULFTA), established in 1918, became a leading left-wing
mass organization. By 1929 its close association with the Communist Party of Canada and pro-Soviet orientation prompted
government surveillance.*

No. 17: Secret Memorandum from C. Starnes, RCMP Commissioner, to the Under-Secretary of State for External Affairs, O.D. Skelton, March 26, 1929, Regarding the Activities of the ULFTA

Royal Canadian Mounted Police
Office of the Commissioner

Ref. No. 175/4511   *Ottawa, 26th March, 1929*

Sir,

It has come to my knowledge that a project has been formed by the leaders of the Ukrainian Labour Farmer Temple Association — which is a thoroughly Communistic body — to send a number of young Ukrainians of revolutionary views to the Ukraine, to be trained there to be agitators, and to return to Canada to "organize" for sundry revolutionary societies, including the Communist Party of Canada.

Another project is under consideration that of sending one of the girls' orchestras maintained at Winnipeg for the purpose of revolutionary propaganda to the Ukraine; also to advance the cause of revolutionary agitation.

As I regard both these schemes — and especially the one first mentioned — as highly mischievous, I take the liberty of drawing your attention to them.

I am sending a similar letter to the Deputy Minister of Immigration and Colonization.

I have the honour to be,
Sir,
Your obedient servant,

[sgd.] CORTLANDT STARNES

Commissioner

The Under-Secretary of State
for External Affairs
Ottawa

No. 18: Secret Memorandum from O.D. Skelton, Under-Secretary
of State for External Affairs, to C. Starnes, Commissioner of
RCMP, March 28, 1929, Regarding the Activities of the ULFTA
[COPY]

Ottawa, 28th March, 1929
Sir,

I am in receipt of your letter of March 26th (No. 175/4511) calling attention to plans of the Ukrainian Labour Farmer Temple Association to send young Ukrainians to the Ukraine for training in propaganda work.

I should be obliged, if this project is carried through, if you could keep us informed of the names of those whom it is proposed to send.

I have a honour to be,
Sir,
Your obedient servant

O.D. SKELTON

Under-Secretary of State
for External Affairs

Colonel Cortland Starnes
Commissioner
Royal Canadian Mounted Police
Ottawa

SOURCE: Public Archives of Canada,
RG 25, Vol. 1492, File: 322 - C

The ULFTA's continued emphasis on its Ukrainian
character placed it at odds with the CPC's focus on revolutionary
class struggle. This tension began to fracture the ULFTA.

No. 19: The Right Danger in the Ukrainian Mass Organizations of
Canada, Statement of the Communist Party of Canada, 1929

THE RIGHT DANGER IN THE UKRAINIAN MASS
ORGANIZATIONS OF CANADA

There are in Canada approximately 350,000 Ukrainians comprising by far the largest single foreign language section of the Canadian working class. At least 90% of all the Ukrainian immigrants are workers and farmers. Virtually all of them are of peasant origin, and previous to the war period of 1914-18 they were employed almost exclusively — as were all foreign born workers — in railroad construction, agricultural work, in the mines, and the rough unskilled labor of the steel industry.

During the past 15 years, however, the role of the foreign born workers in Canadian industry has been changed to a marked degree. With the expansion of industry, they have been drawn with increasing rapidity into all branches of manufacture including the most highly skilled operations. Today foreign born workers predominate in many of the larger industries, and particularly in the so-called "new" industries such as automobile, electrical apparatus, rubber, artificial silk, paper manufacture etc.

And among the foreign born workers Ukrainians occupy an extremely important and strategical position. Firstly, they are the most active and the most highly organized of any language group of foreign born workers. The Ukrainian Farmer-Labor Temple Association a mass non-party organization in close association with the Communist Party embraces more than 5,000 of the most active elements of the Ukrainian workers and extends all over the country. Secondly, the Ukrainians have a strong and very effective press, and thirdly, because they come mainly from the oppressed provinces of Poland, and Roumania, and the Carpathian district of Czecho-Slovakia, they have (collectively) contact with the workers of nearly all nationalities of Central Europe.

Ukrainian workers therefore hold a key position in the general picture of the foreign born workers in Canada, and are a decisive factor in the task of reaching these foreign born workers with revolutionary propaganda and agitation.

Development of Right Tendencies

In the eleven years of its existence the U.L.F.T.A. of Canada has become a powerful institution. With the growth of its influence among the foreign born workers, and particularly of course its authority among the Ukrainian masses, the class hatred of the bourgeoisie against the Communist Party and all its supporting organizations, naturally from time to time found expression in vicious attacks upon the U.L.F.T.A. These attacks took the form of violent denunciations in the bourgeois press, denunciations by politicians in the Canadian Parliament, open support (both financial and political) to the reactionary Ukrainian organizations and priests, petty persecution in matters of licenses for halls etc., etc. From time to time there is a wave of persecution against all foreign born workers' organizations in Canada which support the Communist Party, and the U.L.F.T.A. being the strongest of all of them, receives attention in proportion to its influence.

The obvious duty of the leadership of the U.L.F.T.A. in reply to these attacks was to mobilize the masses of foreign born workers for self-defense, and launch a political counter offensive. But instead of following this obviously correct policy, the leadership (all Party members) adopted a policy of systematic retreats.

Starting with press articles denying the connection of the U. L.F.T.A. with the Communist Party and emphasizing its purely cultural and educational nature, a series of retreats brought them to the point where the national anthem (Canadian) was rendered at occasional entertainments of the U.L.F.T.A. and even to the point where on a day of capitalist celebration (the 60th Anniversary of the Confederation of the Canadian Provinces) the national headquarters of the U.L.F.T.A. at Winnipeg, were decorated in Red, White and Blue, the national colors of Canada.

In the initial condemnation of the systematic deviations the Polcom [Political Committee] of the Party was with one exception (the Secretary of the National Ukrainian Fraction Bureau) a unit. With development of the general struggle against the right, however, the leadership of the U.L.F.T.A. rapidly integrated with the right wing majority of the Party and became one of its most important bases. Factional documents and slanders against the Party's minority were circulated among the Ukrainian workers including even non-Party members of the U.L.F.T.A. A veritable reign of terror was initiated among Ukrainian members of the Young Communist League, and the most unscrupulous methods were utilized to prevent the Party Minority from reaching the Ukrainian rank and file. As a result of these factional measures the Ukrainian members of the Party became consolidated against the Minority, and for the Majority against the line of the Sixth Congress of the Comintern.

The significance of this and its effect upon the work of the Party, is best understood when it is considered in relation with the strategic position of the Ukrainian workers in the ranks of the foreign born. Opposition to Minority comrades in responsible Party positions led very often to opposition to Party policies and hindered the most vital activities. Such for example, was the case in the campaign to organize automobile workers. Here factional opposition to the national organizer of the campaign, resulted in sabotage and open opposition in the most important automobile centre of Canada.

The Struggle Against the Right Danger Among the Ukrainian Masses

The previous Minority has now the leadership of the Party, and the fight to liquidate all vestiges of right opportunism is in full swing. By mobilizing the masses to fight for the streets and the legality of our Party, by aggressively taking leadership of spontaneous strikes and by initiating strikes and organization movements, the present leadership is forcing the

Rights out into the open, and winning the rank and file. But in this process we are singularly handicapped among the Ukrainian Party comrades, and the Ukrainian workers in general.

This is not because of any real political opposition on part of the rank and file. On the contrary, the Ukrainian workers are among the most active and militant workers of Canada. It is because we have not yet been able to reach the Ukrainian rank and file effectively, so as to liquidate the antagonisms (and in many cases subjective opposition) created during the inner Party struggle.

During the election of the Political Bureau of the new Central Committee, the Minority objected to the nomination of Comrade Popovich, (who along with Comrade Nawisisky has been a dominant figure in the U.L.F.T.A.), on the grounds of his open right wing position, and that we held him chiefly responsible for the unscrupulous factional activities of the Right Wing among the Ukrainian leadership. As a result of our categorical opposition, the rights withdrew the name of Popovich. We were then faced with the impossibility of getting another Ukrainian comrade in his place. For several months we were unable even to have important Party documents and circulars translated into the Ukrainian. And having no Party press in the Ukrainian language independent of the press of the U.L.F.T.A., we were unable to carry on an effective inner Party campaign, such as would completely liquidate all confusion.

One of the imperative tasks confronting the new leadership of the Canadian Communist Party is that of revamping and energizing the Party work among the Ukrainian masses. Of the more than 5,000 workers organized around the U.L.F.T.A. only 400 are members of the Communist Party of Canada, and such has been the policy of the leading Ukrainian comrades, that this 400 looks to the Central Committee of the U.L.F.T.A. for leadership, more than to the Political Bureau of the Party. Although the rank and file are excellent revolutionary material, the policy of the leading Ukrainian comrades has been to maintain Party membership at a small minority. Hitherto the Party leadership has accepted this point of view. In addition, there is a strong tendency to consider Party work as consisting primarily (in some places solely) of directing and controlling the U.L.F.T.A. In fact, the U.L.F.T.A. frequently receives first consideration.

This must all be changed. Aggressive organizational work and inner Party educational work must be initiated among the Ukrainian rank and file, and their membership must be built up more in keeping with their numerical strength and influence in the general radical movement.

But the basic task of the Party in its work among the Ukrainian masses is a two-sided task. We must raise the political level of our own Party members and thereby develop a critical political approach by them to their peculiar "Ukrainian" problems and tasks, and to their leadership. Side by side with this must be developed the sharpest self-criticisms in the higher organs of the Ukrainian mass organizations, and the drawing of new youthful elements into the leadership.

Neither side of this important task will be easy. The U.L.F.T.A. and its auxiliary organizations, already represents a large property interest built up by the sacrifices of the Ukrainian working masses and spreading from the Atlantic to the Pacific Coast. Fear of governmental persecution, confiscation of property, fear of illegality, and particularly a certain "superiority" that has developed in certain circles of the membership, all provide a base for the Right Wing, and a fertile source of new Right Wing tendencies. This will increase the difficulty of the fight. But against this we have the fact that among the Ukrainian workers in Canada, the USSR and Soviet Ukrainia are today truly "Stars of Hope", and their Socialist Fatherland. The best and most active among them are determined defenders of the Soviet Union against all capitalist attacks and are unshakable adherents of the Comintern. And this in the final analysis [————].

SOURCE: Archives of Ontario,
MS 367, Reel 6,
Records of Communist Party of Canada

No. 20: Results of the Meeting of the Party Fraction of the ULFTA on February 13th 1930, Statement of the Political Committee of the Communist Party of Canada

STATEMENT OF THE POLITICAL COMMITTEE ON THE RESULTS OF THE MEETING OF THE PARTY FRACTION OF THE ULFTA ON FEB. 13th

1. The Party fraction of the ULFTA Convention, at its meeting of Feb. 13th, defeated a motion to accept the statement of the Political Committee on party policy in the ULFTA by a vote of 80 to 6. Following this, a resolution submitted by the fraction Bureau against the statement of the Political Committee was adopted by a reversal of the previous vote.

2. The discussion in the fraction on the statement of the Political Committee, both at this meeting and the previous meeting of Feb. 9th, expressed in the most violent form, the opposition of the leading Ukrainian comrades to the line of the Political Committee. This discussion and the subsequent decisions of the fraction revealed the following important facts:

a. That the Ukrainian membership of the party constituted a firmly knit federation within the Communist Party of Canada. That this federation sets its loyalty and its discipline higher than the discipline of the party.

b. That the Ukrainian federation within the party categorically rejects the policy of the party, while screening its opposition with empty phrases. That the Ukrainian federation has not followed the policy of the party and today is embarking upon a policy of struggle against the party policy, in defense of the more and more flagrant opportunist line of the Ukrainian leadership.

c. That the Ukrainian federation within the party has become a centre of slander against the party, striving to demoralize the party ranks and discredit the leading party committees, and functionaries.

3. The Political Committee views these matters in the light of the fact that the majority of the Ukrainian members of the party are revolutionary workers, who can be won for the Leninist, revolutionary line of the Party against the opportunist tendencies of the Ukrainian leadership.

4. This makes essential a whole series of measures upon the part of the party leadership in order to develop the struggle against opportunism among the Ukrainian party members, utilizing the lessons and experience in the struggle against the Finnish "Federationists". This important problem must therefore be one of the important questions of the forthcoming plenum of the CEC [Central Executive Committee].

5. Before the plenum, it is necessary for the DECs [Department Executive Committees] to commence at once to utilize the materials issued by the agitprop [agitation propaganda] Dept on the Party organization and structure, for an intensive enlightenment campaign among the Ukrainian party members, particularly, as well as all other members of the party.

6. The Political Committee reaffirms its stand on the statement issued to the Ukrainian fraction and attached herewith, and calls upon all party committees and organs to endorse this stand and carry out in the firmest manner, the policy outlines therein, taking severest measures against all opportunists vacillators, and winning the membership for the policy of the party.

SOURCE: Archives of Ontario,
MS 367, Reel 6,
Records of the Communist Party of Canada

Relaxation of Canadian immigration laws enabled a new wave of Ukrainian immigration to arrive from Europe during 1925-30. As participants and witnesses to the revolutionary upheaval in Ukraine, they were imbued with a strong sense of national purpose. They militated for the idea of a politically restructured Europe in which a consolidated Ukrainian state would have both sovereign and legal rights. Their decidedly European orientation, as expressed in the editorials of their press organ **The New Pathway,** *was seen to be politically imprudent by those who feared that such posturing would place the community in jeopardy.*

No. 21: *Editorial,* Path of Liberation — Path of Struggle, **Новий Шлях (New Pathway),** *No. 1, October 30, 1930*

PATH OF LIBERATION — PATH OF STRUGGLE

[........]

Current events in Western Ukraine demonstrate that the compromising politics of the Ukrainians under Polish occupation will not alleviate the problems faced by the Ukrainian people, but will only help the enemy to successfully denationalize and eliminate the nation. To conduct conciliatory politics with the enemy [........] will reduce the Ukrainian nation to serfdom. The League of Nations and other international organizations are merely foreign branch offices of large countries whose concerns are self-oriented and whose statements deceive the minorities.

Has the League of Nations settled many issues for the benefit of any national minority? [........]. No, they have helped no national minority. [........]

We, Ukrainians, cannot place our hopes on any international institution. Our hope must lie in our own strength. Conciliatory politics with the enemy has been proven unsuccessful because, not only will he not compromise, but continues to intensify his efforts to destroy our nation. Therefore, there remains one path—the path on which we must fight for the liberation of Ukrainian lands from the hands of the occupier. Only by fighting and through political tactics not characterized by servility can we form an Independent Ukrainian State.

Responsibilities of Canadian Ukrainians

We must morally and materially support all those Ukrainian national political groups which are not practising the politics of servility, but are directly waging a political war of liberation; we must support with all our strength Ukrainian national fighting units which are physically waging a battle for liberation with the enemies of the Ukrainian nation — this is the greatest responsibility of every Ukrainian who finds himself beyond the borders of his homeland.

Regardless of one's political affiliation or religion, every Canadian and American Ukrainian who strives for both the liberation of Ukrainian lands and the creation of an Independent Ukraine must remember that "when misfortune befalls the native land, forget your father, forget even your mother, go and fulfill your obligation."

Purpose of our publication

It is the duty of our publication to occasionally remind the Ukrainian community in Canada about this obligation because, as we all know, there is often a tendency to forget or take it for granted.

Wrapped up in party or religious politics which often reach beyond the limits of fanaticism, Canadian Ukrainians waste much time, energy, money and paper on tasks of lesser importance, while [........] not valuing the issues and responsibilities which are before every member of the Ukrainian community in Canada.

Our publication will try to help every member of the Ukrainian community in Canada to put aside his blinders for a moment when the homeland cries out for help; it will encourage the Ukrainian community in Canada to morally and materially support our brothers in our homeland who either politically or physically are waging the war of liberation with the enemy which seized Ukrainian lands; it will help Canadian Ukrainians, citizens who will actively participate in every aspect of Canadian political and community life [........].

We believe that our call to help our brothers in need — those who wish to free our homeland of foreign occupation — will not be wasted but will remind every member of the Ukrainian nation in this land that he must fulfill his obligation to his nation and native [Ukrainian] land.

We believe that we, Canadian Ukrainians, are capable of not only waging party struggles amongst ourselves but, in unison, help those fighting for Ukraine's freedom and [........] defend our rights in this land.

SOURCE: *Новий Шлях*
(New Pathway), No. 1,
[Translated from Ukrainian]

News of famine in Soviet Ukraine pressed the Ukrainian-Canadian community to issue non-partisan appeals to Canada's Prime Minister, R. B. Bennett, and to other foreign heads of state, urging political intervention and assistance in famine relief. Wishing not to upset the balance of diplomatic relations, the issue of famine in Ukraine was treated as an allegation, despite official evidence to the contrary, and the appeals were summarily dismissed.

no help

No. 22: Petition of the Ukrainian National Committee to the Rt. Hon. R. MacDonald, Prime Minister of Great Britain, October 2, 1933, Requesting Investigation of the Famine in Ukraine and Assistance to Organize Famine Relief

October 2nd, 1933

Right Honourable Ramsay MacDonald
Prime Minister of Great Britain
London, England

Sir:

We are taking the liberty of directing your attention to the deplorable fact that for a considerable time the population of Eastern Ukraine (now under a military Bolshevik occupation) are being systematically starved by the Moscow authorities.

The tragedy of the great famine of 1921-22, when nearly ten million people died from hunger, is being repeated, but in all probability on a still larger scale. Thousands of letters are being received in Canada continuously, containing gruesome details of the vast number dying; there are settlements in Ukraine where only one-third — sometimes only one-fourth — of the original population are still alive.

Crop failure is not the reason for this famine, but the brutal policy of the Moscow rulers who, needing grain for export to balance their budget, pitilessly take everything from the farmers, already proletarized. Especially in Ukraine, where the peasants are opposed to the foreign Russian rule, are they being deprived of literally everything, being left without even the smallest ration for daily meals, under the excuse that they are hiding food. With such tactics, even a bumper crop, of huge yield, could not save these people from starvation.

Having in mind the tragic plight of their compatriots, and realizing their moral duty in the matter, the Ukrainian National Council in Canada turn to you, as to a leader of a great civilized nation, with an urgent request to take the necessary steps to arrange for an immediate neutral investigation of the famine situation in Ukraine, with a view to organizing international relief for the stricken population. Any private action, even on the largest scale, would prove inadequate owing to the magnitude of the calamity. We are prepared to supply you, if necessary, with original documents and information giving details of the famine conditions.

We trust that your Excellency will take this, our appeal, under most serious consideration.

We remain,

Yours faithfully,
UKRAINIAN NATIONAL COUNCIL IN CANADA
By:

Chairman of
Advisory Board
[sgd.] L. BIBEROVICH

President
[sgd.] S. SKOBLAK

Secretary
[sgd.] J. M. BOYDUCK

SOURCE: Public Record Office, Great Britain, FO 371/17247

No. 23: Reply from the High Commissioner for the United Kingdom to the Ukrainian National Committee, March 2, 1934, Regarding the Famine in Soviet Ukraine

Office of the High Commissioner
For the United Kingdom
Earnscliffe
Ottawa

2nd March, 1934

Sir,

I am instructed by the Secretary of State for Dominion Affairs to acknowledge the receipt of your communication of October 2nd last addressed to Mr. Ramsay MacDonald, relative to the famine situation in the Ukraine.

His Majesty's Government in the United Kingdom are unable to undertake any action with a view to investigating conditions in territories under the control of the Soviet Government, or to organizing relief for the inhabitants in the absence of any indication that such action would be acceptable to the Soviet Government.

Mr. Thomas understands from His Majesty's Principal Secretary of State for Foreign Affairs that a number of appeals for action in connection with the alleged famine in the Ukraine were, last September, addressed to the Council of the League of Nations by various Ukrainian organizations. It was then decided by members of the Council that the only course which appeared to be open to the petitioners was for them to address themselves to the International Red Cross or to some similar organization of a purely non-political character.

In view of the Canadian status of your Council I am forwarding copies of your communication and of this reply, to the Canadian Government.

I am, Sir,
Your obedient servant,

The President
Ukrainian National Council   [sgd.] W. H. CLARK
Flora Avenue & McKenzie St.
Winnipeg, Man.

SOURCE: Public Record Office,
Great Britain, FO 371/17247

Lord Tweedsmuir's remarks were perceived as official legitimization for ethnic distinctiveness within Canada. Circulated widely, they heartened the organized Ukrainian community.

No. 24: Lord Tweedsmuir's Visit to Ukrainian Canadians, Fraserwood, Manitoba, September 21, 1936

Mr. Bachynsky, Mr. Wawryko and citizens;

I thank you most warmly for the way you have received me today. I do not think that anywhere I have gone in Canada I have been welcomed with a more beautiful ceremony; your escort, your old national ceremony of presenting me with bread and salt and, if I may be allowed to say so, the beautiful and well chosen words of your address. I realize that my welcome is due to the fact that I represent your King, and it will be my pleasure to convey to the King the cordial greetings of the Ukrainian people of Canada.

I am very happy to be among you today. I am among people who have behind them a long historical tradition, for it was your race which for centuries held the south-eastern gate of Europe against the attacks from the East. I can well imagine that this country is home to you, for these wide prairies are very like the great plains of south-eastern Europe from which you came. During my tour of the prairie I have come across many of your people, and I am glad to see that in short time you have come to be a vital element in Canadian nation. You have played your part in the Great War. Today I find your sons in the permanent and non-permanent militia. Wherever I go I hear high praise of your industry and hardihood and enterprise, even under the most difficult conditions. You have become good Canadians.

Every Briton and especially every Scotsman must believe that the strongest nations are those that are made up of different racial elements. The Ukrainian element is a very valuable contribution to our new Canada. I wish to say one thing to you. You have accepted the duties and loyalties as you have acquired the privileges of Canadian citizens, but I want you also to remember your old Ukrainian traditions — your beautiful handicrafts, your folksongs and dances and your folk legends. I do not believe that any people can be strong unless they remember and keep in touch with all their past. Your traditions are all valuable contributions towards our Canadian culture which cannot be a copy of any one old thing — it must be a new thing created by the contributions of all the elements that make up the nation.

We Scots are supposed to be good citizens of new countries, that is largely because, while we mix well with others and gladly accept new loyalties, we never forget our ancient Scots way, but always remember the little country from which we sprang. That is true of every race with a strong tradition behind it, and it must be so with a people with such a strong tradition as yours. You will all be better Canadians for being also good Ukrainians.

Я бажаю вам всім щастя і здоровля.

SOURCE: Archives of Ontario,
G.R.B. Panchuk Collection

*In 1935, a major split occurred within the Communist Party of Canada when leading members of the Ukrainian contingent came to question the excesses of Stalinism in Soviet Ukraine. Leaving the Party and its affiliate, the ULFTA, they still remained committed to the idea of a socialist state structure in Ukraine but one that was politically independent. They conducted a vigorous campaign in their press organ, **Truth,** condemning Stalinism and denouncing its supporters in Canada. As an alternative to the ULFTA, they created a Ukrainian-Canadian working men's association, the Ukrainian Workers' League.*

No. 25: Editorial, *Postyshev has Departed,* Правда (Truth), *March 31, 1937*

POSTYSHEV HAS DEPARTED

[........]

Postyshev's removal from Ukraine, where he was absolute dictator from January 1933, and his demotion to the position of party secretary of a Russian oblast has greater political significance than it would at first appear. This is not the transfer of some ordinary government official or party bureaucrat but the personal emissary of Stalin who has been tossed on the political trash heap. The man who has disappeared from the political horizon in Ukraine played the same role as Stalin does in all of the USSR. Only because Postyshev was Stalin's emissary did he avoid the sad fate of those who would be in his place. To have accused Postyshev of being a "counter-revolutionary," or "trotskyist" and "fascist agent" was not possible because it would have compromised Stalin himself. It was for this reason Postyshev was simply demoted from his position of secretary of the Central Committee of the Communist Party (Bolshevik) of Ukraine, as well as dictator, to that of a secretary of a party oblast committee. But this is the end of the political career of Postyshev and more importantly a slap in the face to Stalin himself.

Postyshev's Four Year Rule — The Greatest Tragedy of the Ukrainian People

The four year rule of Postyshev in Ukraine is the greatest tragedy in the existence of Soviet Ukraine and one of the greatest tragedies in all of Ukrainian history. It was precisely during Postyshev's reign in 1933 that the peasantry in Ukraine massively died of hunger — not the result of drought or some other natural calamity but the consequence of misguided political interference in agriculture. To teach the peasantry "a lesson," the regime under Postyshev's authority refused to give the hungry any assistance. Under the direction and on the command of Postyshev "the 1933 destruction of nationalists" was to follow, when thousands of Ukrainian cultural workers — scholars, writers, journalists, teachers, artists and others — (communists as well as non-party members) were arrested, the only reason being their Ukrainian birth. Without trial they were shoved into prisons, sent to dig canals, to concentration camps, or murdered outright [........].

Truly, Postyshev can be proud of his record [........] on his conscience rests the deaths of millions of Ukrainian peasants who died of hunger.

Postyshev has departed but this should not be taken as an indication that the situation in Ukraine has improved. His departure only shows that no methods of the Stalinist regime which are used against the Ukrainian people, even the most horrible and barbaric, can give the desired results. Although the Ukrainian nation is being squeezed from all sides, as in a vice, they still resist Stalin's henchmen as much as they can. Mass disaffection is growing everywhere and lets itself be heard. And at the height of this unrest they removed the dictator who led the entire apparatus in order to try still other methods of bureaucratic rule. But these changes in personnel and methods will not help them. Only when Ukrainian workers and peasants in association with the working intelligentsia decide their own future will they be able to create their own government and will Soviet Ukraine truly become a Ukrainian worker-peasant state.

* * *

The removal of Postyshev from the position of dictator in Ukraine places in a ridiculous position those Ukrainian lackeys of Russophilism in Canada who spit on all that is Ukrainian and praise all that is foreign. They always declared that Stalin and Postyshev never erred. They labeled Postyshev as the "leader of the Ukrainian people" although he did not even know how to speak Ukrainian. They wrote and spoke of those who pointed out the faults and crimes of Postyshev as enemies of Soviet Ukraine. Soon after, Postyshev disappeared. Gone was the idea that he was "faultless." Even his embroidered Ukrainian shirt did not help him. What will those bought, villainous souls say now, who for a few coins became renegades of their own people? What will all the Navizivskyi's and Shatulskyi's say, who knelt before Postyshev? Truly, this is the unenviable fate of villains and plunderers....

SOURCE: *Правда (Truth),*
March 31, 1937
[Translated from Ukrainian]

The prospect of another world war placed the question of Ukrainian independence on the international agenda. As British subjects, Ukrainians in Canada attempted to convince authorities that the geopolitical interests of Great Britain and the Dominions necessitated support for Ukrainian sovereignty. As a nationalist body, the Ukrainian Nationalist Federation envisioned itself as a natural exponent of the Ukrainian cause.

No. 26: Letter from W. Kossar, President of the Ukrainian National Federation, to O. D. Skelton, Under Secretary of State for External Affairs, June 9, 1939, Arguing that Ukrainian Independence is in the Interests of the British Empire

Saskatoon, Sask.

Dr. O. D. Skelton
Under Secretary for External Affairs
Parliament Buildings
Ottawa, Ont.

Dear Sir:

In recent months, and particularly during the visit of Their Majesties in Canada, I was requested by many persons, both of Ukrainian and Anglo-Saxon origin as well as some Ukrainian organizations throughout Canada, to bring to the attention of the Government of Great Britain and the Governments of the British Commonwealth, the importance of the Ukrainian problem as it is seen by the Ukrainian Canadians.

Since the British Government has made certain definite commitments in Eastern Europe, I take it as my duty as a British citizen to point out some factors in connection with the situation in Eastern Europe and, in particular, in connection with the Ukrainian problem, as the full understanding and solution of that problem may go a long way towards bringing about a political stabilization in that part of Europe.

As president of the Ukrainian National Federation of Canada and the past president of the Ukrainian War Veterans' Association and at the same time as a British subject, I take the liberty of explaining the Ukrainian Canadians' viewpoint with respect to the situation in Eastern Europe.

[........]

As a result of the aggressive policies of Germany and Italy, the Western democracies are deeply concerned about their own position and prestige in Europe. Hence, an attempt on their part at a common anti-aggression front including Poland and Russia.

Poland, which internally is fundamentally unsafe on account of bitter opposition of 7.5 million oppressed Ukrainians and which externally is directly exposed to an immediate danger, had finally decided to entrust her fate to the democracies in the belief that she is gaining a good deal and losing next to nothing. As a result of their alliance with Poland, Great Britain and France may find themselves under an obligation to participate in another world war, a war not of their own choice. And what will happen to Poland in case of such a war? Those who know conditions in that country are certain that a war will bring in its wake an internal revolution in Poland which in turn may eventually bring about a complete collapse of Poland as a state. Unjustly oppressed and unwisely abused and dishonoured the Ukrainian people will not resist the temptation of retrieving their liberty which they have lost as a result of the Polish invasion of Ukraine in 1919.

The U.S.S.R. apparently is safer than Poland, owing to its geographical position and its territorial vastness. In reality, however, Russia is a conglomerate of peoples kept together by a regime based on hatred, distrust, suspicion and tyranny and in consequence is a picture of political impotency, weakness and prostration in spite of its huge army and powerful military equipment. The government has an army and arms but has no certainty against whom the arms will be directed after the same will have been released from the armouries into the hands of the soldiers. At the same time, the 36 millions of Ukrainians in Russia, who live in the territory where the next armed conflict undoubtedly will take place again, are already doing everything in their power to seize the opportunity again as they did it in 1917 for the purpose of seceding from Moscow. The only difference between the present situation and 1917 is that in 1917 the Ukrainian leaders and the common people blamed the czarist regime almost exclusively as the cause of all the evils that had befallen Ukraine. The progressive leaders of Russia in the eyes of the Ukrainians then were free of such blame and the belief of the Ukrainians in their good will and liberalism was strong. Today the Ukrainian leaders as well as the common people fully realize that the present Communist government in Moscow, its democratic declarations notwithstanding, is at least as oppressive as the former czarist government, if not more so, each government treating Ukraine as a colony to be exploited only by the central government in the interests of Russia and to the detriment of Ukraine. The Ukrainians, therefore, are determined and well organized to fight for their independence at any price. This is well known to Moscow. The Russian

Government, as well as that of Poland, exists in a chronic conflict with its own people. The Communist rulers of U.S.S.R. realize that only by preserving the present status quo they may prolong their tenure in office. Should the war come, despite all this, Soviet Russia will be torn to parts by the internal forces, and this will happen as soon as the population will get arms in their hands. The Ukrainian people will play a leading part in this process, exactly as they did 20 years ago, as they will not wait till Moscow arranges for another artificial famine in Ukraine.

The Soviet Russia is in no sense stronger than the czarist Russia. Both are characterized by a complete lack of democracy and political freedom. The czarist Russia was an ally of Great Britain and France during the last war but that war was lost to the allies on the Russian frontier and the czarist Russia collapsed as a result of participating in the war. A similar collapse may be foreseen for the Soviet Russia in any general war in which it may be engaged. An alliance with Russia, *with its present internal situation unchanged,* may prove a source of weakness instead of a source of strength. In any event, the British government after having made commitments in Eastern Europe should be fully acquainted with all the facts in that part of the world and I may humbly add that the failure to see the importance of the Ukrainian problem, which is closely connected with the political situation in Poland, Russia, Roumania and Hungary, may have disastrous effects in time of an armed conflict affecting those states.

I may summarize my points as follows:

1. Russia and Poland, as well as Roumania and Hungary, as presently constituted, each with its huge national minorities of which the predominant is the Ukrainian minority, are negative rather than positive forces in the present international situation; they will become positive forces only after a just solution of the problem of the Ukrainian minority is arrived at.

2. No positive solution of this problem is imaginable without a right of the Ukrainians to the greatest measure of self-determination logically leading to the establishment of a Ukrainian independent state.

3. The establishment of the Ukrainian republic in 1918 was a step in the right direction. Had this republic been preserved with the assistance of Great Britain and France, there would have been no necessity for a Munich in 1938 and there would be no cause for the present anxiety of the democratic states to get the Soviet Russia on their side.

4. The failure to solve the Ukrainian problem will aggravate the present unsatisfactory situation in Eastern Europe by leaving one of the danger spots in Europe.

5. The Ukrainian Canadians are naturally very sympathetic to the fargoing and positive solution of the Ukrainian problem in Europe but they consider it their duty not only to their racial sympathies but also to their British loyalties to bring this problem to the attention of the British Government once this government has made commitments in Eastern Europe. They are of the opinion that the solution of the Ukrainian problem will be in the interests of the British Empire, the greatest stabilizing force in the present world.

I remain, Sir,

Yours very respectfully,

[sgd.] WLADIMIR KOSSAR
President, Ukrainian National
Federation of Canada

SOURCE: Public Archives of Canada,
RG 25 GI, Vol. 1896, File: 165 - Part I

Split into a number of competing organizations, Ukrainian-Canadian nationalists were forced by international circumstances to search for a means of putting forward their common interests. Their purpose was at least two-fold — to reaffirm their ethnic identity and to lobby for the creation of an independent Ukrainian national state.

No. 27: Letter from V.J. Kaye, Director of the Ukrainian Bureau (London), to I. Danylchuk, Secretary of the Ukrainian Self-Reliance League, February 18, 1940, On the Need to Form a Ukrainian National Council in Canada

27, Grosvenor Place
London, S. W. 1

February 18th 1940

I. Danylchuk, Esq., The Secretary
The Ukrainian Self-Reliance League
401, Main Street, Saskatoon, Sask.

My dear Danylchuk,

Thank you for your letter of January 23rd. I expect you had the opportunity to read and to be conversant with the contents of my letters written to Mr. Lazarowich in which I tried as amply as I could to elucidate the situation in London.

Events in Europe require very close observation. As I mentioned in my letters to Mr. Lazarowich, Ukrainians within the British Empire may be faced, in the near future, with extremely important tasks. It would be wise to be prepared for such eventualities. Ukrainian Canadians may be called upon

(1) to act as a link between European Ukrainians and the Allies and to interpret their desires;

(2) to co-ordinate those desires to the general line the Allies may intend of taking in Eastern Europe;

(3) to bring about a collaboration with already existing National Councils of Poland and Czechoslovakia;

(4) to submit clear-cut propositions for collaboration with the mentioned National Councils.

Ukrainian Canadians must do their best to be able to secure well in advance the possibility to be represented at the Peace Conference either as a member of the Ukrainian Delegation or as Advisory Body on Ukrainian Affairs with the British Delegation.

There is little time to be lost, I assure you. Otherwise we may be left out altogether. I am particularly anxious to prepare ground in London, and as far as it goes, I do not see any obstacles why we should not succeed in obtaining at least a fully recognized status. The situation would be greatly facilitated if the Ukrainians would form a National Council as other Nations did and, would start organizing preparatory work for the eventualities which may set in. The formation of such a Council would be officially announced in Ottawa and in London. Delegates would immediately obtain the status of Representatives instead of Observers.

I very well understand the difficulties in forming such a National Council in Canada. I also fully appreciate the objections put forward by the Self-Reliance League to co-operation with organizations which in the past made moves not in accordance with the policy which should have been taken by British Ukrainians [Ukrainians in Canada]. As you know, I had no hesitations in pointing out what I regard as a grave point of weakness in what must (to succeed) be a Common Front. The Self-Reliance League was in position at the outbreak of the War to assume the leadership and to become the initiator of the National Council. I am afraid, the opportunity has been lost, although not entirely. But that does not alter the situation. We are faced with two alternatives, either to try to come to some understanding with existing other groups — (notwithstanding the differences), or to give up the hope of forming a National Council, representative of all Ukrainian Canadians (with the exception of those still professing any Communist creed). The Council which has been formed by the National Federation and the SHD [United Hetman Organization] is not a representative body, no matter what it is called, if the Self-Reliance League chooses to stay out of it. But the same applies to the League [Ukrainian Workers' League]. Both bodies, on the other hand, taken together, would represent Ukrainian Canadians.

You will understand, I am sure, the difficult position of your representative in London. In submitting statements to the press I have to take great care not to have them counteracted (however unvoluntarily) by the representative of the National Federation. At the same time I have to watch carefully that he should not undertake any such steps which would call for counteraction by us. I must say he fully appreciates the situation. There was only one way to eliminate the danger, viz., to make a "gentleman's agreement" and to ask him to notify me about intended statements to the press or to other persons. In cases which required the expression of opinion of ALL Canadians — we had to make identical statements and on one occasion the document (to a Visiting Delegation of France) had to be signed jointly, otherwise it would have been inacceptable.

Fortunately, I am in the advantageous personal position of having connections of long standing which date from the time when I was officially representing the Ukrainian Parliamentary Representation in England, and through my position as Director of the Ukrainian Bureau. But that again does not alter the present situation.

I know that the representative of the National Federation brought the matter to the knowledge of his Executive at Saskatoon. In the common cause, he was good enough to allow me to see his letter on this point. The possibility of collaboration ought not to depend upon any mutable personal factor such as the present compatability of character and upon total suppression of even-legitimate personal aspirations of two individuals. And if the individuals were changed or if the two groups dictated to their delegates two contradictory policies, the cause would at once be disunited here. It would become unintelligible to the Allies. It would be discredited by the Democracies. At such a critical time, we simply cannot conscientiously afford to risk such an avoidable disaster. It is weakness at the most critical period of our modern history, just when, above all, we must all work loyally to assure the triumph of both our old and new motherland. I hope the National Federation may recognize the wisdom of approaching you to remedy the difficulties.

[........]

Enclosed please find the copy of a letter which I sent to the Polish Winnipeg paper *Czas* in reply to their article of January 9th. It explains itself. For your information: my article in *Free Europe* has been written by me as a private person at the suggestion of English circles, and in conjunction with the delegate of the National Federation, in order that responsibility should be divided. It has to be born in mind that Poland is a member of the Alliance and that the Allies would like to have full record between the nations threatened or attacked by eastern aggressors. It is imperative to take a line in these matters and to show our understanding of the situation. If we do not show enough foresight, the question may be settled over our heads, unilaterally, just as it was settled once before. Policy is one thing and sentiment is quite another. It may be creditable and agreeable but it is both very unwise and very unfair on the cause that we Ukrainians should allow natural *sentiment* and impatience outweigh a realistic and *prudent* policy. By self-control and full comprehension of the *underlying* reasons of each new move, we must be on guard against this tendency in ourselves if we are to win.

I shall keep in constant touch with you.

With best wishes

Sincerely yours,

[sgd.] V. KISILEVSKY

SOURCE: Public Archives of Canada,
MG 30 D2/2, Vol. 3, File: Kaye

Unable to overcome their factionalism, Ukrainian-Canadian organizations were brought together by the Canadian government into one national umbrella group — the Ukrainian Canadian Committee. Ukrainian organizations oriented toward the Soviet Union were excluded.

Tracy Philipps, a British civil servant dispatched to Canada at the behest of Lord Halifax, was perhaps the principal architect of this body. He was also a fervent advocate of "Canadianization" — a curious philosophic position which stressed the importance of melding old-world concerns with the new-world political culture. He believed that only a genuine commitment to the principles of liberal political democracy would guarantee the social and political integration of Ukrainians and others into the Canadian mainstream.

No. 28: Report of T. Philipps to the National War Services Department, January 8, 1941, Containing Observations and Recommendations which Concern the Ukrainian Community in Canada

Tracy Philipps
8 January, 1941

SUBJECT

TOUR IN WESTERN CANADA, NOVEMBER - DECEMBER 1941

[........]

VI. Some principles involved in achieving Canadianism

(1) Unification of New Canadians and elimination of their discords.

In constructive diplomacy as in bone ailments, there are two main methods. The first *method* is the most spectacular, prompt and popular. It is the equivalent of a surgical intervention. It often requires other operations to follow. It is rapid, drastic and aggressive. One attacks the foreign element which has entered the body-politic. In the realm of diplomacy it takes the form of threat and direct action. It is a regrettable wartime technique extended to the realm of the civilian. This, in effect, is the only method which, in the time allowed, could be used to unite the half dozen discordant groups of Ukrainians in Canada. It is the least satisfactory method. In these cases the permanence of the cure depends on the period and quality of the subsequent nursing. It is by this less desirable method that the Ukrainians of Canada were got united within a week of the writer's first contact with them.

(2) *The second technique* is the method "convenient to Nature".

This seems the better one, for the future. One gives the subject access to the sun. It illuminates, it enlightens and it heals. One unearths their misapprehensions and their grievances. One treats these simultaneously and sympathetically. One lets in light and air. This second process calls for far more patience. It is slower but surer. It produces a healthy, firm and lasting build-up. The secret sources of inferiority-complex disappear. A modest self-confidence is created. The subjects spontaneously begin to detach themselves from their ancient backgrounds. They no longer huddle together in conflicting clans or in politically ancestral groups. They begin to find all they need in their new country. They are caught up into Canadianism of which at last they can be helped to feel themselves the co-creators.

[........]

IX.

(1) Apart from the Teutonic-speaking peoples, until such time as these eastcentral European peoples (Latins and Slavs) become Canadianized, the nature, and indeed the essence, of the work of Canadianization remains in the realm of *constructive* diplomacy. It is of necessity still part of the Foreign Affairs (of the still foreign peoples) of Canada. Ought one not then to visualize a process of building-in of a richly diversified human material into a very distinctive British-American edifice, identical with neither but drawing the best from both?

(2) If, in our gardens, we wish to transplant successfully from abroad an adult shrub, we are careful in the process not to insist on tearing at once all the old earth from its roots. Indeed, on the contrary, the more we can temper the shock and the set-back of the upheaval by ourselves admitting some of its old and familiar soil to the new hole, the more sure we can be that the tree has something to use as a stabilizing basis to thrust down strong roots into the new land. So far from trying to exclude the old soil, it is the old soil of their old virtues and arts which can best be blended as the basis of the transition to Canadianism. And the more durable the tree, the more gradual the growth. Only more plants can be expected to adapt themselves and to flower in a day. The peasant peoples of Eastern Europe are the most deeply rooted of all the human trees in the world. For them, the shock of transplantation is far more cruel than we know.

(3) Only the most cruel conditions of Nature and of Police-government can wrench them out of the ancestral soil so laboriously fructified by their fathers. [........] That is why here they continue so long to look back over their shoulders to their suffering kindred in Europe whom they hope to help. [........] most of them appreciate (more than do we who were "born free") the rights and liberties of a new kind which they find in Canada. It is surely for us to teach them how properly to use these rights and to realize their consequent responsibilities. Nor can we blame these New Canadians for their appreciation of these liberties. It makes them want, like most democratic peoples, to see freedom, and these blessings of ours, available to their oppressed kith-and-kin in their Old Countries which they have left. In this, they are, after all, our missionaries. And it is in the nature of missionaries sometimes, in good faith, to err by excess of zeal. And, in order to 'save' their families whom they have left behind, converts are notoriously more zealous for the faith than those who are born in the cult.

(4) If we desire that these peoples shall cease to look back over their shoulders to Europe (as, for example, Norwegian-Canadians, Czech-Canadians and even other Canadians are now doing), it is up to us to offer a new embrace to replace the patriotic and maternal mysticism of the Old Motherland.

(5) But what are now the real sense and new values of what we continue to call "democracy"? After this war, on their return, the feet of the young men will be at the door of the old democracy. Having paid the piper (and Hitler), it is they who will call the tune. Meanwhile, the best we can do is to seek to preserve the *principles* of our institutions under new and reinforced forms which will be able to stand up to the gale of the fresh wind which will sweep the world.

SOURCE: Public Archives of Canada,
Tracy Philipps Papers,
MG 30 E 350, Vol. 1, File: 16

*The anti-government agitation of the ULFTA led to a ban
on this organization, the internment of its key members, and the
confiscation of its properties. Once the Soviet Union had allied
itself with the United Nations — but also partly due to public pressure
— this policy was reversed. It heralded a resurgence in the
political activity of a reconstituted Ukrainian-Canadian Left.
Canadian officials, however, remained skeptical about those
whose activities were seen as conforming to the dictates of a
foreign government.*

No. 29: Constitution of the Ukrainian Association to Aid the Fatherland, July 26, 1941

CONSTITUTION

[........]

1. The name of the Association shall be "Ukrainian Association to
Aid the Fatherland". For purposes of convenience it will hereinafter be
referred to as the "Association".

2. *Aims and Objects:* To furnish all possible aid and assistance to our
Fatherland, the Soviet Ukraine, in its present struggle against fascist aggression and in conformity with all national and local laws and regulations.

3. To organize all Canadians of Ukrainian origin for the purpose of
assisting and co-operating with the Canadian Government in furnishing
all possible aid to our adopted land, Canada, in its war against nazi Germany, fascist Italy and their allies.

4. To defend and safeguard the democratic cause against all external
and internal enemies.

5. To organize and conduct irrevocable opposition to all enemies of
Canada and to all enemies of the Ukraine and particularly against Ukrainian fascist, Hitler agents and fifth-columnists who are now busily engaged in activities detrimental to Canada.

6. To organize and foster cultural activities as a means of cementing
fraternal relationship between Canadian Ukrainians and generally the
Canadian people. Such cultural activities may be in the spheres of Ukrainian music, drama and such like activities.

[........]

SOURCE: *Constitution of the
Ukrainian Association to Aid the
Fatherland* (Toronto: n.p., 1943)

No. 30: Memorandum from L. B. Pearson, Assistant Under-
Secretary of State for External Affairs, to the Under-Secretary of
State, N. Robertson, October 12, 1941, Commenting on Canadian
Communist Participation in the War Effort

[COPY]

October 12th, 1941

MEMORANDUM FOR [THE] UNDER-SECRETARY OF STATE

The participation of Soviet Russia in the war as our ally has created certain problems in our relations with that country and with communists in Canada. It seems to me illogical and unwise to approach these problems as if the situation were precisely the same as it was before June 24, 1941. True, Russia did not enter this war to help us but to defend herself; true also, that the sudden discovery by communists in Canada that the war is not imperialistic, but holy, is somewhat nauseating. But the fact remains that whatever the reasons may be, the Russians are fighting on our side and the communists have become ardent protagonists for an all-out war effort.

This being the case, why should we ban Russian war pictures, and, more important, should we keep communists interned when their views toward the war which necessitated such internment must now have changed.

As long as Russia is in the war, there is not likely to be any danger to the security of the state by their release. Representations for such release have been received from the internees themselves and from friends and sympathizers outside. In all cases, the point is stressed, *ad nauseam,* that these men should be freed so that they can fight the Nazis. Naturally, no mention is made of the fact that they were interned because they refused to fight those same Nazis.

A letter from T. G. McManus, who claims to be writing as spokesman for Camp "H" to the Prime Minister, dated October 1st, is typical of the argument that has been used, and will be used to an even greater extent, for release.

McManus, supporting a petition for release, states:

    1.   That no charges of sabotage, spying or subversive activities have ever been presented at hearings granted them, and that they are interned because "representations have been made" that they have been members of the Communist Party of Canada or associated with such members. In no instance has evidence of an overt act been presented against them.

2. That several petitions declaring loyalty to Canada have been presented to the Minister of Justice without effect.

3. That anti-Fascist internees pledge their support for a policy of struggle against Fascism.

4. That they are prepared to fight against any obstruction standing in the way of the most complete possible war effort, and they believe that the labouring people of Canada can be stimulated to "greater marvels of production and sacrifice".

The government should, I think, decide what policy is to be adopted towards the release of these communists, as agitation to this end is likely to grow.

Would it be feasible to release those who are willing to sign a recantation of their previous views towards the war and give a written assurance that they are now willing and anxious, as Canadians, and without reference to Russia — to do their part in the struggle against Nazi Germany?

[L. B. PEARSON]

SOURCE: Department of External Affairs,
History Section, File: 11327 - 46

The Soviet Union's realignment after 21 June 1941, on the side of the Western Allies, precipitated a crisis in the Ukrainian-Canadian nationalist community. It forced them to reaffirm their loyalty to Canada. Yet the government viewed their allegiance as ambiguous and maintained its monitoring of the community.

No. 31: Secret RCMP Report, September 30, 1941, Concerning the Ukrainian National Federation

[COPY]

ROYAL CANADIAN MOUNTED POLICE
OFFICE OF THE COMMISSIONER
OTTAWA

Ref. No. D 945-1-Q-39 (10)   September 30, 1941
      D 945-2-M-2 (2)

SECRET

Dear Judge Davies:

Replying to your letter of the 12th instant, I have no objection to letting Professor Simpson see the report on the First National Eucharistic Congress of Eastern Rites which was submitted by our Special Constable Petrowsky, provided, however, that the identity of the reporter is not disclosed to him.

2. I enclose copy of a further report submitted by Special Constable Petrowsky dealing with the Eighth National Convention of the Ukrainian National Federation of Canada, which was held in the City of Winnipeg during the latter part of last month.

3. You will be most interested in the main resolutions passed by the Ukrainian National Federation and its subsidiary organizations expressing loyalty to Canada and the British Empire. While we have no doubt that the resolutions expressed the attitude of the official leadership of the organization, there is no guarantee that the sentiments have the unanimous approval of the rank and file of the organizations. In this connection, please note the concluding remarks of our reporter.
[........]

                                          Yours sincerely,
Enc. 1.

                                          S. T. WOOD

      The Honourable Mr. Justice T. C. Davis
            Deputy Minister
      Dept. of National War Services
            Supreme Court Building
            Ottawa, Ontario

                          * *
                            *

REPORT

RE

EIGHTH NATIONAL CONVENTION OF THE UKRAINIAN
NATIONAL FEDERATION OF CANADA AND
THE AFFILIATED SECTIONS

The conventions of the Ukrainian National Federation and its affiliated sections were held on *August 28, 29 and 30, 1941,* at the UNF branch hall, 260 Dufferin Ave., Winnipeg, Man.

[.........]

In connection with this convention, a fact must be stressed that *this convention was not planned to be held this year but in 1942,* in view of war conditions, but [also] due to recent international events which created serious dissensions within the ranks of the UNF and disagreement with the policies of the national executive relative to these events and the Ukrainian question in Europe, the leaders of the UNF decided to hold the convention this year, in order to explain their attitude on various questions and 'iron out' the differences in the opinion.

[.........]

An Open Meeting Session on August 29th

[.........] *Rev. Dr. W. Kushnir,* president of Ukrainian Canadian Committee, [.........] delivered the official welcome address on behalf of that body. In this address, Dr. Kushnir declared that Ukrainians in this land enjoyed to the full freedom and privileges of Canadian citizenship and have adopted Canada as their motherland. "It was their duty therefore to unite and coordinate all their efforts to defeat terror, force, and the menace of enslavement of mankind by the ruthless enemy, who has already under his domination many countries in Europe".

W. Kossar was another prominent speaker. He pointed out that one of the important questions before the convening delegates was how to best assist, by a united effort, in the successful prosecution of the war. Speaking of the aspirations of the Ukrainian people in Europe to a complete independence, he stressed that the Ukrainians will stand for no puppet government regardless of any power that would attempt to form on their native soil.

[.........]

Important Decisions of the Convention

I. The national executive of the UNF was empowered by the convention to carry on an intensified information campaign among the English-speaking peoples and the Government circles with regard to all current events and matters relative to the Ukraine and the liberation movement of the Ukrainian people. This action is to be carried on through the medium of the Ukrainian Canadian Committee. Stressing the importance of the moment, the convention has also charged all central organs as well as members of the UNF and the affiliated organizations to inform the Ukrainian community of the developments of international events that are related with the Ukraine and her people, so that "apathy and despair should not spread among the Ukrainian Canadians as a result of harmful tendencies, expressions and opinions of various anti-Ukrainian factors, or even of the uninformed foreign government circles".

II. The next important decision concerns the intensification of the war effort among the Ukrainians by giving full moral support to the recruiting campaign and other war services. In this connection, it was stressed that a great many members of the UNF, the Ukrainian Nationalist Youth, and the Ukrainian War Veterans Association, already serve in various branches of the Canadian Army. Enlistment in the Home Guards and eventual formation of Ukrainian sections in the Home Guards are stressed in the resolution.

III. The Churchill-Roosevelt Atlantic Declaration has been thoroughly debated and it was agreed that, in spite of the fact that the Declaration is "very general" in its meaning, nevertheless it was based on a principle of freedom of nations, expressed in the Second and Third points. Therefore, the Convention has approved a resolution in support of the Churchill-Roosevelt Declaration, and at the same time expressing a hope that in the event of a British victory the Ukrainian question will be taken into consideration in the spirit of Justice and to the benefit of the Ukrainian people in Europe.

IV. A decision to increase aid to the press organ of the UNF, *The New Pathway*, and to transfer the publication from Saskatoon to Winnipeg.

V. The delegates have been instructed to report as well as comprehensively explain the findings and decisions of the convention to members of the local branches of UNF and the subsidiary organizations.

[........]

Notes on the UNF Convention

(Note: The following information was discreetly obtained from several authoritative Ukrainian leaders in Winnipeg.)

1. INFORMATION OBTAINED FROM WASYL SWYSTUN

[........]

Swystun was very frank in disclosing the fact that the Soviet-Nazi war and other international developments reflecting on the Ukrainian question in Europe, have created serious confusion, misgivings, apathy and even misunderstanding amongst the leaders of the UNF and the members of the ranks on the issues of policy and attitude toward certain questions arising from these international events. Therefore, the leaders of UNF had no other alternative but to call a convention immediately in order that the conflicting issues should be explained and policies re-defined in accordance with the views on the matter maintained by the executive leaders.

I inquired from Swystun what, precisely, were the conflicting questions which had so upset the state of minds of UNF members. He said the following were the most disturbing questions:

(a) *Why does Prime Minister Churchill not make any mention or clear cut declaration with reference to the Ukrainian question in Europe?*

(b) *What position are the Ukrainians in Canada to take towards the Soviet-Nazi war in view of the British-Soviet alliance and in the face of such other questions affecting the Ukrainian people in Europe? How to compromise the apparent hatred existing for Soviet Russia amongst the Ukrainians in the light of the British-Soviet accord?*

(c) *What attitude are the Ukrainian Canadians to take towards events taking place in the Ukraine, especially in the case when a Ukrainian puppet government should be formed there under the protection of Nazi Germany?*

Tactfully pressed for further elaboration of these points, Swystun explained that "there were a great many members in the UNF who do not see things the way the leaders do" and therefore dissatisfaction with the present policies of the leaders was noted in many sections. As for the leaders themselves, Swystun added, they were united in the opinion on differing questions, resulting from the international events, with particular reference to the Ukrainian question in Europe. Thus, the leaders of the UNF have not been confused by these conflicting problems as they perfectly understood the complicated situation with all its implications with respect to the Ukrainian question, and as such maintained a consistent policy and direction in the UNF, which were compatible with the loyalty to Canada and the British war aims. With these things in view, the convention was held in order that direct contact with the representatives of the UNF branches be made, conflicting views and issues explained and re-defined, a uniform policy formed, so that the delegates might go home and bring about a proper understanding and re-adjustments within their respective branches, Swystun declared.

In this connection Swystun added that he was the man who acted as the spokesman of the national executive in referring these questions before the convention. Therefore, the convention has accepted the views of the leaders as well as passed appropriate resolutions on all issues in question which approve adherence to the following line of policy:

(a) *Endorsation of principles embodied in the Churchill-Roosevelt Eight-Point Declaration in a belief that these principles will also be applied in the solution of the Ukrainian question in Europe.*

(b) A position that the Soviet-Nazi war does not alter in any way the loyal attitude of Ukrainian Canadians towards Canada and the Empire.

(c) An increased participation in Canada's war effort in the hope that the Ukrainian Canadians will thereby have a voice, with the Government of Canada, in pleading the case of their compatriots in the homeland at the end of this war.

(d) A stand that Great Britain is not in a position to make any declaration with regard to the Ukrainian question due to a number of obvious reasons.

(e) A decision to endeavour to organize a "Free Ukrainian Movement" in London and in Canada in the event a German-inspired Ukrainian "puppet government" is established in the Ukraine, subject to approval by the Ukrainian Canadian Committee and the British Government.

In referring to paragraph "(e)", Swystun stressed that this information was confidentially given and therefore not to be divulged to anybody. He added that this was a closely guarded secret of the UNF national executive and the Ukrainian Canadian Committee until the proper time arrives. The general public must not know of this decision at the present, Swystun explained. This secret resolution of the UNF was discussed with Prof. Simpson, Swystun stated, and he had approved the stand taken. The Ukrainian Canadian Committee has also approved this proposed step in a special meeting called for that purpose on Saturday, August 30th, Swystun said. However, he expressed a doubt as to whether the British Government would agree to the idea of the Ukrainians forming a "Free Ukrainian Movement" along the principle of Free French, Polish, and other similar allied government organized in London, due to the anomalous position the Ukrainians occupied in Europe and the problematical course of British foreign policy regarding the Ukrainians.

[........]

Furthermore, Swystun disclosed that the Ukrainian Canadian Committee had discussed at a special session the principal questions which were incorporated in the resolutions of the UNF convention, including the one referring to a "Free Ukrainian Movement," and that a proper telegram was worded and sent to Prime Minister Churchill and King, President Roosevelt and to the Department of External Affairs at Ottawa. The telegram, Swystun intimated to me, contained an expression of views of Ukrainian Canadians regarding their present stand in the face of recent international events as they concern the Ukrainians in Europe. I was unable to obtain from him any satisfactory answer as to its contents.

2. INFORMATION OBTAINED FROM DR. T. DATZKIW
SECRETARY OF THE UKRAINIAN CANADIAN COMMITTEE
AND NOMINAL LEADER OF THE HETMAN ORGANIZATION

[........]

In brief, Dr. Datzkiw disclosed to me the following information relative to the UNF convention:

(a) He admitted the fact that the Ukrainian Canadian Committee had discussed at its recent meeting the question of a possible Ukrainian puppet government which might be set up in the Ukraine by the German occupants as well as the attitude the Ukrainian Canadians should take towards it. As a result of this discussion, the UCC has formulated a secret plan designed to be put into action when and if such a situation will really be created in Europe. In that case the UCC has decided to approach the British and Canadian Governments with a proposal to set up in London a Free Ukrainian Movement, patterned on French, Polish, etc., "Free Governments", in order that the Ukrainians may join other defeated nations in the struggle against the German domination and for independence of the Ukraine. In this connection Dr. Datzkiw added that the UCC was not quite certain as to what attitude the British Government would take towards this proposal, in view of the fact that London is known to treat the Ukrainian question as a part of Polish and Russian domestic affairs. Therefore, the UCC has its own misgivings in the matter and is quite uncertain as to the course it would follow in the event London turns down the Free Ukrainian Movement plan.

Dr. Datzkiw asserted that as far as he was aware he did not think that the foregoing plan had anything to do with the UNF convention, or that it was instigated by the UNF leaders. However, he had failed to enlighten me as to who had raised this question at the meeting of the UCC, which fact strengthened my conviction that Swystun's version on this subject was correct. The secrecy of this plan was also strongly stressed by Dr. Datzkiw.

(b) Dr. Datzkiw also admitted that the UCC had discussed at its recent meeting various questions arising from the Soviet-Nazi war and the Churchill-Roosevelt Declaration which had a direct bearing on the Ukrainian question in Europe as well as on the attitude of Ukrainian Canadians. Consequently, the Committee had drawn up an appropriate pronouncement on these matters which served as a basis for telegrams that were sent to Ottawa, London and Washington. My informant disagreed again with my suggestion that this telegram and the discussion on these matters at the meeting of the UCC were inspired by a resolution dealing with identical subjects that was passed by the UNF convention and which might have been submitted to the UCC for approval and action by

Swystun or some other member[s] of the UCC, who at the same time are officers of the UNF.

(c) At this juncture, I asked Dr. Datzkiw a number of questions concerning the UNF, namely: Were the leaders of the UNF sincere in their declarations of Canadian loyalty? What about the link between the UNF and its parent organization, the Organization of Ukrainian Nationalists, whose headquarters is in an enemy country? What would be the attitude of the UNF in the event the OUN leaders, whom all UNF members recognize as their own, should head a puppet government of the Ukraine? To these questions he replied as follows:

There can be no doubt as to the sincerity of the UNF leaders and most of its members in their declaration of Canadian loyalty and in activities on behalf of Canada's war effort. Come what may in Europe, the UNF will remain faithful to Canada, even in the event their acknowledged leaders in Europe are installed by the Germans to head a puppet government of the Ukraine. However, he admitted, it might be expected as natural that a certain section of the UNF members would be swayed by such an event and therefore sympathize with a Ukrainian puppet government. The idea of Ukrainian independence was dear to every Ukrainian, no matter under what conditions it existed, and this must be taken into the account, Dr. Datzkiw added. As far as the UNF connection with the OUN leadership was concerned, he explained that *Col. H. Sushko*, representative of the OUN, had visited Canada in 1938, in connection with the annual convention of the UNF, advising the leaders of the UNF to adopt the policies of their organization in accordance with the national policies of the country of their allegiance, namely to follow a pro-Britain line of policy in the event of war, regardless of what attitude the leaders of the OUN make take in Europe, or what events may follow there. Thus, Dr. Datzkiw explained, the UNF is keeping in line with this policy to this very day, as it is considered the most consistent with the interests of the people and their allegiance to the British Crown.

Dr. Datzkiw added in conclusion that in his opinion the UNF carried on its activities in full co-operation and understanding with the Ukrainian Canadian Committee, in the same manner as other Ukrainian organizations, which are members of the UCC, and that all Ukrainian organizations are in full agreement on all cardinal questions relative to Ukrainian Canadians and the Ukrainian question in Europe.

[........]

3. INFORMATION OBTAINED FROM DR. M. MANDRYKA

Dr. M. Mandryka, member of Ukrainian Canadian Committee and a Socialist in his convictions, frankly admitted to me that he knew little about the recently held UNF convention. However, he had willingly

disclosed certain interesting facts about the UNF and its leaders which
have a direct bearing on the convention as well as throw new light on the
subject matter thus far discussed. In brief, he disclosed the following:

(a) The Ukrainian Canadian Committee held a luncheon-meeting on
Saturday, August 30th, in honour of Prof. Simpson of Saskatoon, in the
course of which important subjects were discussed, the most important of
which concerned the question of British war aims in the light of the
Churchill-Roosevelt Atlantic Declaration as it affects the Ukrainian question in Europe. This discussion had drifted into such a hectic stage, when
some members of the UCC had raised the question of lack of any stand in
British war aims regarding Ukrainian aspirations in Europe, that one of
the members, Dr. B. Dyma, picked up his hat with the evident intention
of leaving the meeting, having been alarmed by the trend in the discussion. Dr. Simpson took a prominent part in the discussion, in the course of
which he declared that the British Government is not in a position to pur-
sue any other policy toward the Ukrainian question than the present and
that loyalty and adherence to British war aims is the only way through
which Ukrainian Canadians may win due recognition and, perhaps, consideration of their plan on behalf of their compatriots in Europe.

Dr. Mandryka added that he also took part in these discussions, at
one point disagreeing with Swystun and several others who maintained
that the Churchill-Roosevelt Declaration means also that the Ukrainian
question will be considered at the conclusion of this war.

(b) According to Dr. Mandryka, the majority of the UNF members
and leaders are at heart enemies of democracy. They pay lip service to
democracy for official consumption but privately they tactfully refute what
the organ of the UNF, the "New Pathway", has said editorially about
democracy. This is the tactic they use in order to spare themselves the consequences during war-time. Their organization is based on totalitarian
ideology, despite claims to the contrary and the evident display of Canadian loyalty and the support given to Canada's war effort. However, Dr.
Mandryka added, a great many of the UNF members are already convinced that the Germans have never been sincere in their attitude towards
Ukrainian aspirations.

(c) Wasyl Swystun, Dr. Mandryka further stated, can be described as
the "hired negro" of the UNF, its "manager" for the duration of the war,
who at present is the most active and shows more initiative than any other
leader of the UNF, both in the organization and in the Ukrainian Canadian Committee. However, the real pillars of the UNF are Kossar, Prof.
Pavlichenko, and V. Hultay. Prof. Simpson, Prof. Watson Kirkconnell,
and Tracy Philipps are, on the other hand, looked upon by the UNF as
"protective shields" of the organization in these difficult times. The UNF
will not do a thing without first obtaining proper advice from Prof. Simp-

son, Dr. Mandryka declared.

(Note: Dr. Mandryka did not bring up the matter of the proposed "Free Ukrainian Movement" decided upon by the UCC, and I did not think it advisable to touch on this matter for an obvious reason).

4. INFORMATION OBTAINED FROM M. STECHISHIN

M. Stechishin, editor of the *Ukrainian Voice* and member of the Ukrainian Canadian Committee, informed me that he knew very little about the UNF convention for an obvious reason. Being a member of an opposing organization, he had no access to the sessions of the convention, he said. However, as an old acquaintance of mine, he freely discussed with me pertinent subjects, therefore his information has some bearing on the recently held UNF convention. He said in part as follows:

(a) The UNF convention was held this year for the purpose of making necessary re-adjustments in the organization in view of its connections in Europe and the international developments.

(b) Asked as to his opinion regarding the sincerity of the resolutions the UNF convention had passed in which adherence to British War Aims, and so forth, was stressed. Stechishin replied that this was the most difficult question to answer for anyone. There was no reason to think the UNF members were insincere in the declarations of their loyalty to Canada, despite the appearances to the contrary, although there may be some among them whose sincerity can be doubted. The fact is, the UNF has not thus far officially severed its connections with OUN [Organization of Ukrainian Nationalists] in Berlin, though the UNF organization is autonomous, whereby it conducts its affairs according to policies of the country to which members of the organization owe their allegiance. In view of the ideological connection with the OUN and the pro-German propaganda disseminated by the UNF in the past, designated to build the hopes of the Ukrainians regarding German aid for Ukrainian aspirations in Europe, the UNF leaders have done a great harm to Ukrainian people, because they have created wrong impressions in the opinion of other peoples about the whole Ukrainian movement.

(c) The UNF representatives in Ukrainian Canadian Committee are noted for erratic moves and propositions of an extreme nature. For example, the UNF delegates have proposed to the UCC at one of its recent sessions that the Canadian Government be urged against its alliance with Stalin, however other members of the Committee have rejected the very idea of such a suggestion.

(Note: It will be noted that Stechishin did not mention anything about the "Free Ukrainian Movement" decided upon by the UCC, or concerning the message sent by it to Ottawa, London, and Washington. Apparently, Stechishin belongs to those members of the UCC who are capable of keeping a secret.)

GENERAL REMARKS

(a) It is my impression that the great majority of the UNF members are at heart wishing for a defeat of Soviet Russia in the hope that the Ukraine would emerge an independent country, regardless of the fact as to who will control the destiny of a Ukrainian government. It is also my belief that a great many of the UNF members would not object to seeing a German-controlled "puppet government" in the Ukraine.

(b) It is also certain that most of the UNF members do not wholly approve of the British war aims on account of the Polish and Russian Alliances as well as the asserted lack of a clear-cut declaration regarding the Ukrainian question in Europe.

(c) In view of these facts, it is possible that the majority of the UNF members had voiced dissatisfaction with the course of policies the national executive was pursuing with regard to these questions, resulting in apathy and a let up in the activities of the organizations, which eventually had prevailed upon the alarmed leaders of the UNF to call the convention, for the purposes of making necessary re-adjustments. The resolutions which the convention had passed, the appeals made at the Convention calling for a greater war effort, and the disclosures made to me by Swystun will illustrate this contention.

(d) It is more than apparent that leaders of the UNF are living in fear for themselves and their organization on account of past pro-Fascist tendencies, the link with the OUN, and the uncertainty of the position in which the organization is regarded by the Authorities. Therefore, it seems as likely, that the leaders and responsible members of the UNO [UNF] are sincere in their patriotic endeavour in the interest of Canada's war effort as the only way to (1) demonstrate their loyalty to Canada, and (2) to anticipate recognition and official favour with the Government in a postwar settlement of the Ukrainian question in Europe.

(e) It may be taken for granted that certain section of the UNF members as well as other Ukrainians in Canada will likely sympathize with a "puppet government" in the Ukraine.

(f) However, it is hardly possible that the UNF or any other similar group of Ukrainians in Canada, excepting the Communist, will cause any serious trouble for the country now or at some critical period in the future.

(g) It is also possible that Ukrainian Nationalists, including the UNF and Hetman followers, will be cured of their alleged pro-Nazi leanings when it will become apparent that Germany is really pursuing a policy of enslavement of the Ukrainians in Europe. A great many Ukrainian Nationalists seem to be already disillusioned in Germany, on account of her recent action in merging Western Ukraine with Poland as part of the German Protectorate.

(h) Finally, taking all this into consideration, it seems that the only logical attitude toward the UNF organization which can be formed at the present moment, is a policy of cautious watchfulness and the accepting of the loyalty and assistance of the UNF in the war effort at face value.

[M. PETROWSKY] Spl. Cst.

Ottawa, September 17, 1941

SOURCE: Public Archives of Canada,
Tracy Philipps Papers,
MG 30 E 350, Vol.1, File: 12

Many Canadians viewed Ukrainian-Canadian commitment to the idea of an independent Ukraine as irrelevant to the war effort and potentially disloyal. The more extreme proponents of nativist sentiment accused Ukrainians as a group which assiduously avoided military service. Ukrainian Canadians pointed to contrary evidence showing that Ukrainians were over-represented proportionately in the armed forces and argued that their views were consistent with those principles for which Canada went to war.

No. 32: Letter to the Editor, *Only Two Sides*, **Edmonton Bulletin**, *March 6, 1942*

ONLY TWO SIDES

Editor, Bulletin: Both Mr. A. de H. Smith and you are to be commended for his splendid letter, "Bomb-Proof Billets," in Thursday's Bulletin. As one living in an alien district, I can realize that it took high moral courage to publish a realistic message of this sort.

Mr. Smith has lost a son; you may have lost some goodwill from the elements in our population definitely hostile to all British traditions, though quick to shelter behind "British justice and fair play." But the political poltroons who are more concerned with winning votes than they are with winning this war, mouth platitudes about "unity" when there is no unity; try to tell us that these people are "loyal" — the Japanese are loyal, the Germans are loyal, the Italians are loyal, the Ukrainians are loyal, Canada's dead must groan in their graves as they consider how Anglo-Saxons have handed away our heritage, go cheerfully to fight in all the far corners of the world, while staying behind are these people who came to a ready-made British freedom which gave them legal protection to vilify us and to sneer at the country which gave them land, food, work, shelter, aid in sickness and in unemployment — how quick they were to rush for relief! — and how slow they are to rally to the colors.

It's time for the truth. We are in a fair way to losing this war. The crew of a single Japanese seaplane took Kieta in the Solomon islands the other day; a score of Canadian riflemen could have held them off. First John Bull was going to save us; now it's Uncle Sam. Perhaps we should try to save ourselves. But we're not going to fight, à la Mr. Hlynka, for the dear old Ukraine; we want to see the aliens here rounded up to fight for Canada. If not naturalized, their own governments are more than welcome to them.

I have said that this is an alien district; and so it is, preponderantly Ukrainian, and not one single man of that race or racial strain has volunteered for the active army from this district.

Mr. Smith suggested some organization. I suggest it be called the Loyal Legion, basically composed of the same sort of people who saved this country in other dark hours when invaders were pouring over the frontier — the United Empire Loyalists. The lines have been drawn very sharp in this war; there are only two sides — those who are for us and those who are against us.

As your editorials say — Think it over!

J. M. GILROY
Northville

SOURCE: *Edmonton Bulletin*,
March 6, 1942

*In mid-1943, responding to Ukrainian-Canadian na-
tionalist claims for international recognition of Ukraine's right to
self-determination, a campaign to discredit such claims was
launched by the Soviet Union. Publications, highly critical of
the nationalist community, were produced for the English-
speaking Canadian public and diplomatic representations were
made to the Department of External Affairs. Soviet representations were of vital concern and treated seriously by Canadian officials because they highlighted the issue of Canada's role as ally.*

*No. 33: Memorandum from N. Robertson, the Under-Secretary of
State for External Affairs to Prime Minister W. L. Mackenzie
King, May 6, 1943, Commenting on Audience with the Soviet
Ambassador who Expressed Concern Over Ukrainian Nationalist
Activities in Canada.*

NAR/SR
6.05.43

MEMORANDUM FOR THE PRIME MINISTER

The Soviet Minister came to see me today...

Mr. Gousev went on to talk about resolutions he had noticed in
Canadian-Ukrainian newspapers, passed by Ukrainian Nationalist
organizations, advocating an independent Ukraine and consequentially
the dismemberment of the U.S.S.R. He said that this attitude of Ukrainian organizations was pro-Fascist, and did not understand why, if we had
a censorship in force, we allowed newspapers in Canada to publish articles
advocating the breaking up of the territories of our ally, the Soviet Union.

I replied that, though the Ukrainians were a very large bloc in
Canada, more numerous really than either the Poles or the Russians, they
were not a factor in influencing Canadian government policy, and too
much importance should not be attached to speeches and resolutions of the
Ukrainian Nationalists. Ukrainian nationalism, like Irish nationalism,
was a pretty sturdy growth. Ukrainian immigrants in Canada were mostly
from the Western Ukraine, territories that had formerly been part of
Austria-Hungary and latterly had been under Polish rule. Their nationalism had, in the years between the wars, been primarily aimed at
separation from Poland though, like all national movements, they aspired
to union as well as to independence. He objected to the Canadian Ukrai-

nian Nationalists undertaking to speak on behalf of 50,000,000 Ukrainians, at least 30,000,000 of whom must be citizens of the U.S.S.R., who
had fought very bravely in resisting the Nazi invasion and who were completely loyal Soviet citizens. He pressed his point about the anti-Soviet articles in Canadian Ukrainian papers, stigmatizing them as pro-Fascist. I
said that undoubtedly there were some elements in the Ukrainian Nationalist movement which could be so described, but that the great bulk of
the Canadian Ukrainians were not in any sense pro-Fascist. We would be
much happier if they would look at the world through Canadian eyes and
think of themselves solely as Canadian citizens, but the process of
assimilation took time. There was no doubt that many Ukrainian Canadians had cherished hopes for the formation of a separate Ukrainian state.

I explained that we were very reluctant as a democracy to use the censorship powers taken under the Defence of Canada Regulations unless the
successful conduct of the war required it. As a matter of policy, the
Government did not invoke the censorship to suppress editorial opinion
however critical it was, even of the Canadian Government. It would be
difficult to apply a different censorship rule to criticisms of Allied Governments. Such criticisms, though often irritating, were not really important
and the use of the censorship to suppress them might well do much more
damage to the general interest than could the offending articles
themselves.

SOURCE: Public Archives of Canada,
MG 26 J4, Vol. 345, File: 3715

*Provided that Canadian security was not jeopardized by
Ukrainian-Canadian activities, government officials were content to remain unobtrusive but watchful. The government identified the division of the organized Ukrainian-Canadian population into a nationalist majority and a pro-Soviet minority as the
most important characteristic of the community.*

No. 34: Secret Memorandum from N. Robertson, the Under-
Secretary of State for External Affairs, to D. Wilgress, Canadian
Minister to the USSR, May 28, 1943, Describing the Political
Situation within the Ukrainian Canadian Community.

SECRET

AIR MAIL

No. 40   Ottawa, May 28th, 1943

The Canadian Minister to the
Union of Soviet Socialist Republics
Kuibyshev, U.S.S.R.

Sir,

I have the honour to refer to our telegram No. 50 of May 22nd, and
to previous telegrams referring to the Ukrainians in Canada. Since the
controversy which is at present taking place amongst various groups of
Ukrainians in Canada appears to have been a subject of comment in the
Soviet Union, it may be of interest to you to receive further details concerning the Ukrainian community here.

The Ukrainian Canadian Committee, to which exception is taken in
the article referred to in your telegrams, was formed in 1940 as a central
federating committee, representative of five Ukrainian organizations. The
committee includes in its membership all the more important Ukrainian
Canadian societies, with the exception of the communist ones which had
been banned at the outbreak of war. Its membership consist only of cor-
porate bodies and not of individuals.

The five organizations which became members of the Ukrainian
Canadian Committee were sharply divided by conflicting policies in the
years before the war. It was only after considerable persuasion on the part
of private individuals, amongst whom were Professor Simpson and Tracy
Philipps, that they were persuaded to unite in a single federating organization. Its purpose was to eliminate as much as possible the friction which
had existed amongst Ukrainian groups and to enlist their support for the
war effort.

The one interest common to all member organizations in the Ukrainian Canadian Committee was their support for the idea of a Ukrainian
National state. This interest has been one of long standing amongst certain sections of the Ukrainian community. It was encouraged during the
period immediately preceding the war by the hope that a German attack

on the U.S.S.R. might result in the establishment of an independent Ukraine. Following the German-Soviet Agreement of 1939, the hopes of the Ukrainian nationalists were raised still further by the assumption that the U.S.S.R. had become a potential national enemy of the countries opposed to Germany.

The German attack on the U.S.S.R., and the subsequent acceptance of the U.S.S.R. as one of the United Nations, has obviously been a considerable embarrassment to the Ukrainian nationalists. They have not been prepared to abandon an objective of such long standing as independence for the Ukraine, but at the same time have been quite genuinely interested in supporting the war effort of Canada and the United Nations generally. They have, therefore, been generally very discreet in their public statements in regard to the Ukrainian question and until recently have avoided any overt comment on the relation of the U.S.S.R. to this problem.

The five member organizations of the Ukrainian Canadian Committee are the Ukrainian National Federation, the United Hetman Organization, the League of Ukrainian Organizations [Ukrainian Workers' League], the Ukrainian Self-Reliance League and the Brotherhood of Ukrainian Catholics. All five are represented amongst the officers and committee members of the federating society.

The most vocal and influential of the Ukrainian nationalist organizations represented on this committee is the Ukrainian National Federation. This organization has its headquarters in Saskatoon and has local organizations in many centres in Western Canada and also in industrial centres in the East. It is apparently in a fairly strong financial position and publishes a semi-weekly newspaper, *Novy Shliakh*. Its president is Mr. W. Kossar, who, for the past fifteen years has held a position of leadership in the organization. Mr. Kossar apparently was a member of the Ukrainian military forces which took part in the struggle for liberation at the conclusion of the last war. In Canada he has been an instructor in the Research Laboratory of Plant Ecology in the University of Saskatchewan. It has recently been announced that Mr. Kossar intends to resign from his post in the University of Saskatchewan and to devote his full time to educational work for the Ukrainian National Federation. An equally influential member of the organization of which Mr. Kossar is president is Mr. W. Swystun, a Winnipeg lawyer, who has shown an active interest in Ukrainian nationalism for some years.

The Ukrainian National Federation has often been referred to as a member of the notorious Ukrainian Nationalist Organization [Organization of Ukrainian Nationalists], the European terrorist society, which under German sponsorship, has been fostering Ukrainian nationalism during recent years. There is no clear evidence of this connection,

although it is probable that some leaders of the Ukrainian National
Federation have had contact with the U.N.O [OUN]. In 1939 Mr. Kossar
visited Europe and it is assumed that in company with Professor Granov-
sky, a Ukrainian nationalist from the western United States, he made contact with U.N.O. [OUN] leaders in Germany. He and Professor Granov-
sky also secured an appointment at the Foreign Office in London on their
way back to this continent. On the occasion of this journey, Mr. Kossar
called at the Department. The record of his interview with Dr. Skelton
would not indicate that he was at that time, either extreme or dangerous in
his nationalism.

Less influential, but more objectionable in outlook, is the United
Hetman Organization. This body supports the claims of Skoropadsky to
sovereignty over an independent Ukraine, and shortly before the war it
sponsored a tour through Canada on the part of Skoropadsky's son. The
United Hetman Organization is authoritarian, both in organization and
outlook. Its leader in Canada has been Michael Hethman, who apparently
arrived in Canada shortly before the war. He carried a commission of
some kind from the parent organization in Europe, which enabled him to
assume control of the Canadian body. Hethman himself has not been in
evidence in recent times and his point of view is represented in Ukrainian
circles by Dr. T. Datskiw, who was at one time his "Chief Commissioner"
and who is now treasurer of the Ukrainian Canadian Committee. The
United Hetman Organization has been weakened by internal dissension
and also by faulty leadership. There are two newspapers which have
generally been associated with this organization. One is *Ukrayinsky Robeetnik* (Ukrainian Toiler) of Toronto and the second is *Ukrayinsky Holos*
(Ukrainian Voice) of Winnipeg.

The League of Ukrainian Organizations [Ukrainian Workers'
League] is probably the least important of the associations forming the
Ukrainian Canadian Committee. Its membership includes a small group
of Trotskyite Ukrainians, who, though communist in origin, are now
hostile to the Soviet Union. They are sometimes known as the Lobay
group, a name derived from one of their principal members.

The Brotherhood of Ukrainian Catholics is the lay organization of the
Greek Catholic Church in Canada. It is almost entirely under clerical con-
trol and it is represented on the Ukrainian Canadian Committee by Dr.
W. Kushnir, who is Chancellor of the Ukrainian Catholic Diocese of
Canada. He is also President of the Ukrainian Canadian Committee.

The Ukrainian Self-Reliance League is also an organization con-
nected with a religious body. It is a lay society within the Greek Orthodox
Church in Canada and its representative on the Ukrainian Canadian
Committee is the Very Reverend S. W. Sawchuk, administrator of the
Ukrainian Greek Orthodox Church of Canada. I gather that the term

"Self-Reliance" in the title of this organization may also be translated as "independence" and may thus express the nationalist outlook of its members. Mr. Sawchuk is Vice President of the Ukrainian Canadian Committee. The fact that his name is associated with those of Dr. Kushnir and Mr. Swystun in the three most important offices of the federating society, is an indication of the attempt made to reconcile the interests of the three organizations represented by these men.

The spokesman for the Ukrainian nationalist organizations in the House of Commons is Mr. Anthony Hlynka, member for Vegreville, Alberta, a community in which many Ukrainians live. Mr. Hlynka is a supporter of the Ukrainian National Federation and has suggested in Parliament that the independence of the Ukraine might become an object of Canadian external policy. It was he who sent to the Prime Minister the memorandum on the Ukrainian question recently prepared by the Ukrainian Canadian Committee, and he also forwarded a copy of the memorandum to this Department. Mr. Hlynka's interest in this question has made him a subject of attack by Ukrainians who are opposed to separation of the Ukraine from the U.S.S.R. He is a member of the Social Credit Party in the House of Commons.

All the Ukrainian organizations which have been named have given admirable support to the Canadian war effort. On a number of occasions leaders such as Mr. Kossar have indicated that their first loyalty of Ukrainian Canadians must be to Canada and that the first objective is to help in winning the war. The meetings of these organizations have been investigated by the R.C.M.P. and their press has been followed closely by the censorship authorities. In spite of their interest in Ukrainian independence, their activities have not given rise to any serious objection since the outbreak of war.

Shortly after the German invasion of the U.S.S.R. there appeared in Canada an organization known as the Ukrainian Committee in Aid of the Fatherland. This committee became successively, the Ukrainian Association to Aid the Fatherland and the Ukrainian Canadian Association. The leadership of this organization is drawn from amongst the former communist societies which were banned after the outbreak of the war. The Chairman is John Horbatiuk and the secretaries are Michael Mutzak and Michael Dushnitzky. The Ukrainian Canadian Association is actively pro-Soviet. It has vigorously attacked the Ukrainian Canadian Committee and its member organizations, accusing them of being fascists and agents of the German government. Within the last year a bitter feud has developed between the Ukrainian Canadian Association and the Ukrainian Canadian Committee, in which each side has accused the other of being under the control of agencies located outside Canada.

The Soviet Minister to Canada, when he called on the Under-

Secretary of State for External Affairs recently, raised the question of the activities of the Ukrainian nationalists in Canada and asked why it was not possible for the censorship authorities to suppress nationalist newspapers which are advocating an independent Ukrainian state.

The principal Ukrainian newspapers to which Mr. Gousev may take exception are *Novy Shliakh* (New Pathway), Winnipeg, *Ukrayinsky Holos* (Ukrainian Voice), Winnipeg, and *Ukrayinsky Robeetnik* (Ukrainian Toiler), Toronto. All three have been consistent advocates of Ukrainian independence and have been unremittingly hostile to the territorial claims and policies of both Poland and the U.S.S.R.

Novy Shliakh, a semi-weekly organ of the Ukrainian National Federation, is the most influential of the nationalist newspapers. It was published originally in Saskatoon, but its offices were moved to Winnipeg shortly after the formation of the Canadian Ukrainian Committee. Generally speaking, its nationalism has been consistent and outspoken, but not inflammatory. Until recently, direct attacks have not been made against the U.S.S.R., though the Polish Government has been the object of severe condemnation on a number of occasions. Within the past few months, however, the tone of the paper has become more strident and its attitude towards the U.S.S.R. less discreet. The probable causes of this development have been the vigorous attacks now being made on *Novy Shliakh* and the Ukrainian National Federation in the columns of the radical publication *Ukrayinske Zhitya* (Ukrainian Life), and the emergence of controversy over the relations between the U.S.S.R. and its neighbours. A recent editorial in *Novy Shliakh* (March 17) illustrates this tendency:

> Yes, the West-Ukrainian territories should belong to the Ukraine, an independent Ukrainian nation. Under an independent Ukrainian nation, the Ukrainian people do not understand the so-called Ukrainian Soviet Socialist Republic undr Moscow, because this republic is a Russian imperialistic swindle, a fiction. Its status in the Muscovite empire, also called U.S.S.R., is the same as that of a woman slave in a sultan's harem. It is the same as the present nationhood of Norway, Holland or Belgium under Hitler.

Certain other Ukrainian journals are both nationalistic and anti-communist, but none is so aggressive in its editorial policies as are *Novy Shliakh, Ukrayinsky Holos,* and *Ukrayinsky Robeetnik.* Sometimes a generally conservative attitude may appear to have wider political implications than are intended. For example, the organ of the youth movement within the brotherhood of Ukrainian Catholics *Budutchnist Natsyi* (Future of the Nation) recently carried an editorial eulogizing Professor Kirkconnell. Opinions on the subject of Professor Kirkconnell have become so extreme amongst Ukrainian-Canadians that praise and blame of his views inevitably appear to be expressions of policy on communism and the U.S.S.R.

Mr. Gousev may take comfort from the fact that the opinions of the Ukrainian Nationalist Press do not go unchallenged. Within the past year two vigorous Pro-Soviet Ukrainian newspapers have commenced publication, one in Toronto — *Ukrayinske Zhitya* and the second in Winnipeg, *Ukrayinske Slovo* (Ukrainian Word). These journals characterize their nationalist rivals as fascist and lose no occasion to denounce both their policies and their supporters. Tho Soviet case in connection with the Ukraine, as well as in more general matters, has been fully stated in these journals and the suggestion cannot be sustained that the Canadian Ukrainians are being presented with only one side of the picture.

Though the editorial columns of the Nationalist Ukrainian Press are often indiscreet, nothing has yet been published which is either subversive or seditious. The Nationalist journals in Canada have probably been more restrained than papers of similar outlook in the United States. The danger at the moment is that Ukrainian papers may be led to take a more provocative line either because of the establishment of an independent Ukrainian Government by the Germans or because of the accusations of fascism which are being made against them in the U.S.S.R. There is also danger in the possibility that anti-Soviet opinion in the United States may encourage a more intransigent attitude on the part of the Nationalist Ukrainian Press on this continent.

As a result of the heightened controversy in the Ukrainian Press on the subject of Ukrainian nationalism, it is proposed that a letter be addressed by the Chief Censors of Publications to the editors of the Ukrainian (as well as other) publications. This letter would point out in general terms and with examples, the methods used by the German propaganda authorities in their efforts to divide the United Nations, and suggest that assistance is being given to the Germans in their propaganda when controversies which divide members of the United Nations are pursued. On the whole the foreign language press in Canada has in the past been very responsive to suggestions of this nature and it is thought that the Censors' letter would result in some abatement of the present discussion.

In regard to your suggestion that a statement should be made in the House of Commons deploring activities and controversies which divide the members of the United Nations, I may say that the occasion for such a statement will be taken if it arises. A statement made which lacked some suitable occasion might well appear artificial and raise questions and misgivings as to the motives by which it was prompted.

It has not been the policy of the Canadian authorities to interfere with the activities of foreign language organizations, provided that they remain within the law. The inadvisability of raising any question in regard to

Ukrainian independence is fully appreciated here and the situation is being watched in the hope that extreme statements on either side can be moderated and arbitrary action avoided. I shall be glad to learn of any further reference to this problem in the U.S.S.R. and shall keep you informed of further developments in Canada.

I have the honour to be,
Sir,
Your obedient servant,

[sgd.] N. A. ROBERTSON
for the
Secretary of State for External Affairs

SOURCE: Public Archives of Canada,
RG 25 G1, Vol. 1896, File: 165 - Part III

Before the end of World War II the Canadian government had established a systematic policy for dealing with the activities of the organized Ukrainian community in Canada. Policy fell under the purview of the Wartime Information Board, the agency responsible for domestic and foreign propaganda.

No. 35: Memorandum from D. Buchanan to J. Grierson, Director, Wartime Information Board, June 4, 1943, Regarding Policy on the "Ukrainian Question"

WARTIME INFORMATION BOARD

MEMO. TO JOHN GRIERSON

UKRAINIAN QUESTION

Following the meeting with George Glazebrook, Malcom Ross and I [D. W. Buchanan] discussed the information and suggestions revealed by him, and this memorandum on background and conclusions is for your information.

Malcom Ross is handing in a separate note on the legal set-up, orders-in-council, etc.

BACKGROUND

No continuity of policy in regard to war information and Canadian groups of Ukrainian origin has ever been established.

Existing agencies of government, that are concerned with this question are:

(1) The Committee of Co-operation in Canadian Citizenship, which has mostly non-governmental representation, and in which the work of Tracy Philipps is centralized. (National War Services)

(2) Press Censorship under W. Eggleston and H. W. Baldwin. (National War Services)

(3) Censorship of Incoming Publications (Foreign), excercised in practice by Dr. Biberovich, working in co-operation with H. W. Baldwin. He also prepares a resumé of Ukrainian Press comment (Canadian) for W.I.B. reports division. Biberovich is a well-educated Ukrainian, held in high regard by Press Censorship and by External Affairs. (Department of National Revenue)

(4) Custodian of Enemy Property (Deputy Custodian, E. H. Coleman K.C.). This bureau is in charge of the seized Ukrainian-Labour halls. (Department of Secretary of State)

(5) R.C.M.P., insofar as they investigate subversive activities. (Department of Justice)

(6) While External Affairs has no direct contact with Ukrainian groups in Canada, it takes an extra-curricular interest in what other government departments do in this regard.

Interesting details on the above are:

PRESS CENSORSHIP

The Ukrainian Press is divided roughly into three main sections:

The Nationalist (advocacy of the Ukrainian state)
The Moderate (including religious papers)
The Left-Wing (Communist in sympathy)

H. W. Baldwin, who has studied their comments, from the point of view of press censorship, reports that while the left-wing press is attacking Tracy Philipps, there is little or no direct mention of his activities in the rest of the press. The Nationalist press, however, has been actively taking up all anti-Russian material, has reprinted verbatim the anti-Communist speech of Watson Kirkconnell, and some of their comments closely parallel items put out by Axis propaganda broadcasts fro Europe. On the other hand, all papers support Canadian participation in the war.

COMMITTEE ON CO-OPERATION IN CANADIAN CITIZENSHIP

Tracy Philipps travels, makes speeches, has personal contacts with editors of Ukrainian papers. Over a year ago, Dr. Simpson, then on this committee, suggested some co-operation with the rural film circuits, but nothing came of this, except in a minor way in Saskatchewan. Philipps made a recent visit to the United States, made speeches, and since has been attacked in editorial comment in some of the American Ukrainian papers.

Glazebrook is preparing a complete brief on the legal set-up and membership of this committee.

WHY THE QUESTION OF UNIFORM POLICY IS URGENT

(1) The anti-Russian attacks in the nationalist press (also in the Polish language press)
(2) The Russian minister has protested
(3) The Ukrainian Canadian Committee (a committee of Ukrainians only, with avowed nationalist representatives as well as several church group representatives) from its headquarters in Winnipeg made a plea for Ukrainian self-determination. This was in petition to the Canadian government.
(4) Various committees on civil liberties have recently passed resolutions protesting the action of the Canadian government in continuing to hold Ukrainian-Labour halls in the custody of the alien and illegal property branch of the Department of the Secretary of State.

CONCLUSIONS

FIRST STEP — to call a meeting of representatives of all departments and bureaus concerned to examine what is being attempted and where matters now stand.

Note — representatives of Press Censorship as well as of the Committee of Co-operation in Canadian Citizenship should attend from War Services.

SECOND STEP — this meeting should be asked to define a uniform policy in regard to the foreign language press in Canada, and it should authorize the formation of a standing interdepartmental committee to implement this policy, with W.I.B. providing the permanent secretary for this committee.

THIRD STEP —   W.I.B. should appoint a Canadian, who is interested in the Ukrainian question, but who has never had definite connections with any one of the several religious and political groups among the Ukrainians, to take charge of this work. This *non-partisan background* is essential.

FOURTH STEP —   W.I.B., working with this committee, should then help the departments concerned to introduce the new policy, and W.I.B. itself should concentrate at once on a study of the foreign language press and the preparation of a service to it.

External Affairs and the Press Censors are already in practical agreement concerning the need for the above four steps.

Glazebrook feels that War Services must, if approached, consent to what is suggested above. There is no suggestion of doing away at once with the Committee on Co-operation in Canadian Citizenship, but if Tracy Philipps began to deviate from the uniform policy laid down by the inter-departmental committee, then of course, his position would become untenable and he would have to resign.

FIFTH STEP —   the question of films and radio projects related to the Ukrainians could be tackled later by the W.I.B. expert, but not immediately because at present it may only be possible to get uniform agreement on steps one to four.

SOURCE: Public Archives of Canada,
RG 36/31, Vol. 13, File: 8-9-2

*Under considerable pressure to moderate its views on the
question of Ukrainian independence, the UCC executive made a
declaration at the First Congress of Canadian Ukrainians which
clearly stated that Ukrainian Canadians were unambiguously
loyal to the Canadian state and its war aims.*

No. 36: UCC President's Introductory Address at the First Ukrainian Canadian Congress, June 22-24, 1943, Winnipeg, Canada, Discussing the Relationship of Ukrainians to Canada and the War

INTRODUCTORY ADDRESS AT THE CONGRESS OF THE UKRAINIAN CANADIAN COMMITTEE

Rev. Dr. W. Kushnir

[........]

The significance of this Congress

Today's Congress, which is being held under the leadership of the
Ukrainian Canadian Committee, the supreme body of the organized
Ukrainians on the American continent, marks in the history of our people
on this side of the ocean, a decisive and a memorable event. That is
evidenced by the presence here of the representatives, the delegates and
the guests who represent the Canadian citizens of Ukrainian descent who
have settled in Canada from coast to coast. If we, furthermore, consider
that those present at this Congress constitute the brain and the marrow of
our people in all their cultural and social aspects, then we may partially
understand and appreciate the significance and the importance of this
Congress. Were this Congress to be convened during ordinarily normal
times, even then its significance would hardly be mundane. But today the
world is far from normal, and human life far removed indeed from regular
daily routine. For at this very moment the whole world is engaged in a
global and total war. Already many peoples have been enslaved, and
many nations have tottered and fallen. Others are nearing exhaustion in
this mighty struggle; and still others are collecting the remnants of their
forces in order to achieve final victory over the common enemy and thus
guarantee for themselves and for the whole of mankind freedom from
tyranny and a safe and peaceful existence. Canada, too, is in its fourth
year of combat with her enemies, the deadly enemies of all mankind. We
firmly believe that from this terrible struggle Canada will not only emerge
victorious but will become stronger and finer than she ever was before.

Deep in our hearts we anticipate and already cherish the coming time when the banners of victory will unfurl over our beloved Canada and its people, the time when the sons and the daughters of our land shall return to their homes crowned with the wreath of triumph. Yet the road to this happy hour is long and arduous. It demands from all citizens the acme of our strength and energy, constant toil and sacrifice, unending vigilance, and ceaseless action. That is why this Congress, being undertaken during such trying times, has such historical significance and importance for us and for our future generations in Canada. I would venture to say that the significance of this Congress is probably greater than we may today realize. It is imperative for all of us to prepare to cope with the highest obligations which are today emerging before us in their full magnitude; it is necessary for us to aspire and to become the men who during the most decisive crisis of mankind were able lo lead their people to a better future.

Cultural Unity with the Ukrainian Race

We, Ukrainian Canadians, identify ourselves culturally with the great Ukrainian race in Europe, but we dedicate all of our strength and all of our abilities towards the sound development of our new homeland, our Canada. That is why this Congress does not mark the beginning of any new endeavor by the Ukrainian Canadians; rather it is a review of what has been hitherto accomplished by us here in Canada, — a synthesizing of what we have contributed to Canada. It is a critical evaluation of the worth of our labors, and thereby a strengthening and a stabilization of their value in the light of present conditions. It will result in a further co-ordination of all our endeavors unto the successful and victorious prosecution of the war in which Canada is engaged. Our Congress is the result of the cultural and moral strength and the vital patriotism of all the Ukrainian people in Canada. It is the culmination of the factors which affected us throughout the half century of our existence in Canada. On this memorable day we feel more strongly than ever our organic unity with the great Ukrainian people in Europe; we feel that their centuries' old traditions weigh heavily upon our shoulders, like the shadows of an immense primeval forest; our hearts respond sympathetically to the noble chord emanating from the age-old history of the Ukrainian soil and its people, engendering in us a melancholic melody that blends with the mosaic of Canada and gives to it that magical force and that beautiful entity which makes of Canada the "Promised Land."

If we consider ourselves still more thoughtfully, remembering that we are the representatives of the multi-thousands of Ukrainian people in Canada, in our hearts there arises a new feeling of hope. After several decades of often-felt hopelessness, amidst a constant struggle against the rather adverse circumstances of our social environment which was marked by misunderstanding and discrimination from varied directions, after decades of internal crisis which promised to result in a fatal and anaemic animosity within our ranks, we Ukrainian Canadians are no longer without hope. Today, we understand and we realize that through the noble efforts of all of us, through an intelligent concentration of our forces for a greater cause, we shall be able to overcome all of our difficulties. And as a hopeful people always act, so do we today organize on a firm basis all of our plans. In our hearts unfolds the bright picture of the just organization of human life both now during the war period, and after the present conflict when our own country Canada, after final victory is won, will realize a permanent and a lasting peace.

In this respect, we Ukrainian Canadians represent a people rehabilitated through our experiences with a serious crisis in our organized life in the past. All danger is now over. Our minds are as clear as the minds of those after a battle, for it is then that the human spirit rehabilitates and regains its normal strength. With this clearness within our minds and hearts, we begin our Congress, — our deliberations about the world in which we are living and which encompasses us in all its varied aspects. Nor will these deliberations be meaningless. They will be exemplary discussions of the Ukrainian people who have suffered a great deal and during a long time, whose sentiments are today turbulently affected by the terrors of a total global war, and who — from behind the ramparts which defend them — contemplate from an experienced viewpoint the fate which faces them and the rest of mankind.

Clarification of the Background of the Life and Actions
of the Ukrainian Canadians

The Ukrainian Canadians, more than any other recent immigrants, labored under the most trying circumstances. Those things which were held dear, worthwhile and patriotic when practised by other peoples — were regarded by certain organs of public opnion as less worthwhile, less valuable and less patriotic when practised by the Ukrainians. It was for this reason that the Ukrainian Canadians constantly experienced discrimination, — as if they were a less desirable element in the Canadian population. We were quite conscious of this. Although this resulted in many less-stable individuals breaking beneath the weight of public opinion, and although in our societal ranks there arose serious tensions, yet we did not permit ourselves to lag behind in our constructive efforts. Practical evidence of this are the hundreds of cultural institutions, — institutions which are not the peculiar fruit of the present war-situation, but which trace their origin back to the beginnings of our settlement in Canada. Practical evidence of this are the efforts of the Ukrainian laborers

and the Ukrainian farmers who have imprinted upon the virgin soil of
Canada unerasable marks of their industry, their prayer, their labor and
their sacrifice. For this the Ukrainians were repaid by a suspicious questioning of their patriotism to Canada on the part of certain irresponsible or
thoughtless Canadian citizens. Even now, the sincerity of the war efforts
of the Canadian Ukrainians is questioned. These sincere efforts to help
our government and nation in this time of emergency, the lives of our
sons, and the sacrifice of what little wealth we possess are still not enough
to spare from further attacks our people and their patriotism.

The fact that we are raising this particular question at the Congress
demonstrates the deep sorrow felt by the thousands and thousands of
Ukrainian Canadians in Canada. Nor are we raising this issue merely to
arouse the sympathy of our co-citizens. This aggrieved feeling of sorrow is
directed towards all the citizens of Canada, towards all organized bodies of
public opinion ... so that they shall know who exactly are their sincere
friends, and who are the secret enemies of their country, their liberties,
and their democratic institutions. Due to the well-prepared propaganda of
these internal enemies many are deluded into thinking and believing that
their enemy is their friend, whereas his main aim is the destruction of the
nation and the country. We, Ukrainian Canadians, who have experienced
many enemy campaigns in the past as well as the present, know how
subversive organizations prepare the groundwork for their own particular
cause, and appreciate how well they can appeal to the opinions of millions
in order to keep them prejudiced unto a just and righteous cause.

We, Ukrainian Canadians, have never belong to this type of people.
Our labors and our sacrifices for Canada during the last five decades bear
witness to this fact. We have never been, we are not, and we never will be
Communists or Nazis ... as certain organs of public opinion would like to
see us represented. Being such is contrary to our nature, contrary to our
traditions, and contrary to the experiences of our people. We are only
Canadians, who are respectfully loyal to our Government of Canada, to
Canada's liberties, and to her democratic institutions. That is why, on this
first day of our Congress, by pledging our unwavering loyalty to Canada
and to our King, we solemnly pay homage to the Government which is experiencing both internal and external difficulties in its stupendous task of
preserving the nation from ruin and of safeguarding its democratic institutions and its traditions of liberty.

The Attitude of the Ukrainian Canadians Towards the Cause of the United Nations

In the present total and global war Canada does not stand alone. She
stands in line and in equal partnership with many larger and smaller na-

tions and countries. The Ukrainian Canadians understand very well that the present conflict will determine the fate of many nations for many generations to come. During this fateful period, the Government of Canada can depend on the Ukrainian Canadians to do their full share so that the war-torn world may soon find peace and order. We, Ukrainian Canadians, will do all in our power to make our people understand clearly, completely and practically the Atlantic Charter, whose principles promise a better future for all peoples great and small; and we believe that at an opportune time these principles will apply also to the Ukrainian soil, and will bring for the Ukrainian people the fulfillment of age-old aspirations: *To be Free and Independent on their own Soil; in a Free Europe, among Free Nations, also a Free Ukrainian Nation.*

[........]

The Objectives of the War

As all other peoples the Ukrainian Canadians long for peace, but not for peace at any price. We long for a peace based on victory and justice. The road to peace is the road to total victory. This is to be a victory not only on land, on sea, and in the air, but a complete and total victory for the ideals of Canada, — ideals which guarantee to all the freedom to worship God, and which respect the personal liberty of every individual and of every nation. [........]

Our Political Principles

Our political principles are identical with the political principles of every honest Canadian patriot. It is true that we, Ukrainian Canadians, have been constantly criticized for our political principles or orientations. That is why we find it necessary to discuss this very important problem both in retrospect and in perspective. We know that the main purpose of the state is the common welfare of the community. We know that the politics of the state is a visible manifestation of the ever-present responsibility of the state for the fate of its people — a constant selection of means through which the state tries to realize its temporary and specific aims. In this respect too, the principles of faith and morality must direct us. That is exactly why the Ukrainians can neither be Communists nor Nazis. They denounce on the spot every totalitarian form of state. And because they know that the political development of any country is the responsibility and the concern of the whole people, the Ukrainian Canadians will, through their own organizations, apply all their energies to have this democratic principle exercise a proper influence in the public life of Canada. We abide by the principles of democracy, and we demand full rights for our working people. We demand our share of the economic, political and social privileges that are our democratic citizen right. We feel a cultural unity with the Ukrainian people, but we honorably fulfil our obligation to dedicate all of our forces and talents to the sound development of our homeland, Canada.

[........]

Ukrainian Canadians and the Problem of a Canadian Nation

Our Congress is indeed a memorable event for the Ukrainian Canadians. The attention of all the Ukrainian people in Canada is directed to it. These Ukrainian Canadians are with us and behind us in spirit, with a resoluteness of which in our life we have not had many examples. This is gratifying to us, indeed. But it seems to me that our Congress has a much more significant meaning which must be emphasized.

The Congress of the Ukrainian Canadians which opened on the 22nd day of June, 1943, is an evident and practical demonstration that the Ukrainian Canadian Committee has been able to consummate one very important task: it has during the three years of its hard work been able to direct the attention of its people away from the smaller and more unimportant problems of everyday life to the larger problems of history, to an increased concern for the fate of the world with which theirs is so inexorably bound. This is a spiritual transformation, an emergence of the Ukrainian Canadians at the very vanguard in the process of the formation of a Canadian nation.

In the mosaic of the different peoples of Canada, this spiritual attitude of the Ukrainian Canadians is the most important contribution which we can offer to Canada and to her sound prosperity. The Ukrainian Canadian Committee has made our people highly conscious of their duties and obligations. Through its constant work, the Ukrainian Canadian Committee has enlightened the ranks of our society, making them realize that not merely economy but politics too decides the fate of our people. All peoples may better their economic standards whenever they are ready to undertake the responsibility for their own welfare, a responsibility based upon the virtuous, pure and unpoluted forces of heart and spirit found in their finest members.

The Ukrainian Canadians until recent times suffered from fraternal conflict. Formerly divided into numerous parties and sectional groups which contended about rather unimportant questions of everyday significance, they are now committed to unity and solidarity, and with this to more responsible endeavors and to more responsible duties towards our Canada. After years of bitter experience, we realize that without unity there is no strength; and without strength, there is no liberty.

We, Canadian Ukrainians, rededicate today our moral forces in a resolve for a better future. Leaving behind all unimportant matters, we enter upon the stage of history. We unfurl our banners with the slogans:

  1. *All efforts of Ukrainian Canadians for the Victorious Prosecution of the War;*
  2. *Peace, Liberty and Honor for All Peoples after the War.*

These are the slogans of a Christian democracy that inherits those basic virtues on which may be normalized the inter-relations among peoples and states, among the rich and the poor, among the big and the small. These civic virtues are being negated today on an alarming scale. The citizen who negates them offends and disrupts the most tender sentiments of his neighbor. How just that often the aggressor himself must pay the price of aggression by losing peace, liberty and honor for himself and for his own people. Only through the preservation and the practice of these democratic virtues can everlasting Peace in Europe and in the World be made possible. May these civic virtues be the slogans of the Congress of the Ukrainian Canadians:

> *For a Victorious Canada: Peace, Liberty and Honor!*
> *For All People in a Free Europe: Peace, Liberty and Honor!*
> *For the Ukrainian Nation, too, among the Free Peoples in a Free Europe: Peace, Liberty and Honor!*

SOURCE: *First Ukrainian Canadian Congress*
(Winnipeg: Ukrainian Canadian Committee, 1943)

Despite their effusive professions of loyalty to Canada, the Ukrainian Canadian Committee's activities were monitored closely by Canadian internal security forces. Such covert surveillance was to continue into the postwar period.

No. 37: Secret Memorandum from R. G. Riddell, [July 1943?],
Providing Synopsis of Secret RCMP Report Entitled First All
Canadian Ukrainian Congress, Winnipeg, June 22, 24, 1943

SECRET

MEMORANDUM
First All Canadian Ukrainian Congress
Winnipeg, June 22, 24, 1943

A detailed secret report, over 80 pages in length, has been received
from the R.C.M.P. on the subject of the All Canadian Ukrainian Congress held under the auspices of the Ukrainian Canadian Committee in
Winnipeg, in June. The following points in the report are of particular interest.

1. The Success of the Conference

It appears that the Conference was regarded as a major success by its
sponsors. There had been considerable opposition to holding it on the part
of prominent Ukrainians and its leaders proceeded in their plans with
some misgivings. The fact that the conference was well-attended and that
it passed without serious incident is therefore regarded as a vindication by
those interested in calling it. The conference was attended by 715 ac-
credited delegates and guests.

2. Political Statements

There is evidence in the report that the conference leaders were concerned to avoid statements or discussions of a kind which would cause embarrassment to the Government or give ammunition to their Communist
opponents, and on the whole they appear to have been very successful in
this regard. The resolutions of the conference, shown on pages 26 to 31 of
the report, are almost wholly unobjectionable in character and the one
resolution referring to Ukrainian Nationalism is very general and guarded
in its wording. During one session of the congress speeches were made on
the subject of Ukrainian Nationalism, but these do not appear to have
been inflammatory, with the possible exception of certain remarks made
by Mr. Hlynka.

There were, however, two incidents which caused considerable
distress to the congress leaders. The first of these was an unguarded
reference by General Sikevich to the Soviet, Polish and Czechoslovak
Legations in Ottawa, and the second was a hostile reference to the
U.S.S.R. by Mr. Hlynka. These statements would provide good material
for anyone wishing to make out a case against the Ukrainian Canadian
Committee but I doubt if either one of them was of much significance.

3. Rivalries Within the Ukrainian Canadian Committee

According to the R.C.M.P. report there was ample evidence at the congress of healthy rivalries and antagonisms amongst the groups represented and their leaders. One body in the Ukrainian Committee, the so-called Lobay group, a former Communist and probable Trotskyite organization of small membership, withdrew from the congress shortly before the opening meeting. The rivalry between the Greek Catholic and Greek Orthodox groups found expression at the congress, and the Nationalists of the Ukrainian National Organization [Ukrainian National Federation] are regarded with suspicion by the more moderate Ukrainian Self-Reliance League.

[........]

4. Relations with the Poles

Resolutions passed by Canadian-Polish organizations and sent to the congress in an attempt to enlist Ukrainian support for the Polish position were a cause of considerable embarrassment to the congress leadership. The congress drafted a resolution of reply which is reported to have been "non-committal".

5. Canadian Representation

Professor Simpson and Mr. Kirkconnell were both present at the congress. Professor Simpson apparently was an official representative of the Minister of National War Services. On one occasion at the congress a message of greeting signed by the Minister was read.

[........]

Mr. Kirkconnell took the occasion to deliver an oration of major proportions. It appears that he spoke for two solid hours and the text of his address occupies 36 pages of the report. His speech, which had many provocative phrases, contained a spirited defense of the Committee on Co-operation in Canadian Citizenship, and a strong tribute to Tracy Philipps. It contains also a denunciation of Fascism, and Mr. Kirkconnell characterizes the government of the U.S.S.R. as "Fascist of the left". He has, therefore, some very unpleasant things to say about the Soviet government under this ingenious classification which I think originated with Tracy Philipps. The speech also contains a discussion of the European-Ukrainian question, which according to the report was not viewed with favour by the members of the congress. Mr. Kirkconnell supported the Polish claims to the Western Ukraine and said that Ukrainian Nationalists must come to some agreement with the Polish government in regard to this area. On the other hand, he said that Ukrainian Nationalism in the Russian Ukraine could find expression only within the Soviet system and by agreement with the Soviet government. The latter part of his address contains a provocative attack on the Communists in Canada and in particular on the Ukrainian Farmer-Labor Temple Association which he says is less than 25% Ukrainian. There are a number of nice phrases such as "yelping members of a seditious organization", well calculated to keep the discussion on a good high level.

6. Ukrainian Language

It is perhaps of general interest that a good deal of attention seems to have been paid to the teaching of the Ukrainian language in Canada and the preparation of textbooks and other material in Ukrainian. It is not possible to estimate how seriously these suggestions are taken, but it would seem that, in the minds of some Ukrainians at least, there is a desire to see Ukrainian given the status of French as an alternative second language.

[sgd.] R.G. RIDDELL

SOURCE: Public Archives of Canada,
RG 25 G1, Vol. 1896, File: 165 - Part III

Canadian officials were convinced that diplomatic recognition of the Ukrainian Soviet Socialist Republic would resolve the Left-Right split within the organized Ukrainian-Canadian community. Such a move was not possible given Britain's lead on the question. Britain's position was influenced by its commitment to the inviolability of Poland's pre-1939 frontier and, to a lesser extent, fear of the decolonialization implications of extending diplomatic status to Ukraine as well as to other Soviet Republics.

No. 38: Secret Memorandum for the Prime Minister, July 4, 1944, Concerning Diplomatic Recognition of the Ukrainian SSR

SECRET
July 4, 1944
MEMORANDUM FOR THE PRIME MINISTER

The United Kingdom Government has recently inquired as to the views of the Dominion Governments concerning the exchange of separate representatives with the Ukrainian-Soviet Socialist Republic, should such a request be made by the Soviet Government (D.O. telegram Circular D-947 of June 29th).

Following the constitutional changes of February 1, 1944, Commissars for Foreign Affairs have been appointed for most of the constituent republics of the Soviet Union. As the Ukrainian S.S.R. is the second-largest of these it is not unlikely that the Soviet Government may make a definite request for an exchange of separate representatives between the Ukraine and the United Kingdom. If such a request is made at all, it may also be addressed to the Canadian Government, since a large proportion of foreign-born Canadians came originally from districts which are now a part, or which are claimed by virtue of plebiscites conducted in 1940 to be a part, of the Soviet Ukraine. Moreover, the Soviet Government has been interested for some time in the existence of Ukrainian nationalist movements which have had some following among Canadians of Ukrainian origin, the purpose of which was to set up a Ukrainian State independent of the Soviet Union.

The United Kingdom authorities feel that it would be difficult indefinitely to withhold recognition of the international status of the 16 republics, that some of the United Nations are likely to grant recognition, that once one country accorded recognition others would follow, and that the position of countries which refused to do likewise would cause great resentment in the U.S.S.R.

The United Kingdom authorities feel, however, that an immediate exchange of representatives with the Ukraine would raise three difficulties:

(1) Such action might be interpreted as recognition of the Ukrainian Republic's claim to parts of pre-war eastern Poland;

(2) It might serve as a precedent for similar action in regard to the Byelo-Russian republic which claims parts of eastern Poland amounting to as much territory as the whole pre-1939 extent of the former republic;

(3) It might also serve as a precedent for a request to exchange representatives with the Baltic States, which, if granted, would involve recognition of their incorporation in the Soviet Union.

The United Kingdom authorities suggest, therefore, that the question of recognition of the 16 Republics should be postponed, if possible, until the peace settlement. At the same time the Commonwealth Governments and the United States should exchange information and consult regarding this question, directly and through their representatives in Moscow.

It is proposed that a reply should be returned to the Secretary of State for Dominion Affairs expressing the general concurrence of the Canadian Government with the course of action outlined by him, and suggesting:

(1) The claim of each Soviet republic to separate representation should be judged upon its own merits. A much better case can be made for the recognition of the Ukraine, which is the world's second-largest Slav

state and holds an important place in world economy, than for the recognition of the Byelo-Russian or of the Kirghiz and Turkmen republics. Moreover, this approach would obviate the necessity of reviving the very undesirable controversy over the alleged analogy between the international status of the Soviet republics and the British Dominions. (The United Kingdom Government points out that the best historical analogy is to be found in the limited international status accorded to some of the larger German states, such as Bavaria, between 1870 and 1914).

(2) While it would be desirable to postpone acceptance of separate representation of the Ukraine until after the peace settlement, the Soviet Government may press the question before them. They may, for example, wish Ukrainian representatives to participate in discussions concerning the reparations payments to be imposed on Germany. Since recognition seems bound to come in any case, it might be more conducive to Allied unity vis-à-vis the enemy states to grant it promptly and without bargaining.

(3) With respect to the Baltic States, their incorporation in the Soviet Union appears inevitable. Recognition of their incorporation seems bound to be granted by the United States and the members of the British Commonwealth. While recognition now runs counter to the policy of refusing to recognize (except with consent of the parties directly concerned) territorial changes made during the war, it is undesirable that this question should become a matter of controversy during the peace settlement, where it might easily serve to sidetrack more important issues, and be exploited to divide the United Nations to the detriment of their permanent interests.

(4) Nothing, however, should be done to hasten recognition, or the exchange of representatives with the Ukraine, or to suggest to the Soviet Government that they would receive a favourable reply if they should ask for it now.

From the point of view of Canada's Ukrainian population, recognition by Canada of the international status of the Ukraine as part of the Soviet Union would be a bitter blow to one section while it would be warmly welcomed by another. In the long run, however, its effect upon the anti-Soviet Ukrainians in Canada is likely to drive from their minds the mirage of absolute Ukrainian independence and in this way to hasten the process of their assimilation. Once the question ceases to be a matter of controversy, it is also to be expected that the most important source of the division among Ukrainian-Canadians will be removed and both right and left-wing elements may be induced to co-operate more effectively in the interests of Canadian citizenship.

[sgd.] N. A. R[OBERTSON]

SOURCE: Public Archives of Canada,
RG 25 G1, Vol. 1896, File: 165 - Part IV

*United States intelligence agencies compiled this descriptive
and comprehensive assessment of the organized Ukrainian community in Canada. Its preparation was dictated by North
American security concerns.*

**No. 39: Secret Internal Memorandum of the Foreign
Nationalities Branch, Office of Strategic Services (OSS), United
States Government, August 8, 1944, Reporting on Ukrainian
Activities in Canada**

SECRET

MEMORANDUM BY THE FOREIGN NATIONALITIES
BRANCH TO THE DIRECTOR OF STRATEGIC SERVICES

Number 205   8 August 1944

THE UKRAINIANS IN CANADA

I. INTRODUCTION

The half-million Ukrainian-Canadians share with their half-million
neighbors of Ukrainian descent in the United States a similar historical
background. Contacts between the Ukrainian groups north and south of
the Canadian-American border are close; events in the Ukrainian-
speaking community of one country are quickly reflected in that of the
other and the Canadian and American Ukrainian-language newspapers
often quote from each other. Ukrainian-American fraternal societies have
small branches in Canada, and lecturers and organizers occasionally exchange visits.

Some Comparisons with the United States: Although the American and
Canadian Ukrainian-speaking populations are about equal in number,
the Canadian group of course is proportionately of far greater importance.
This is true not merely because Canada's population is one-tenth that of
the United States, but also because of a far greater concentration, especially in the western provinces of Manitoba, where the Ukrainian-speaking
community is numerically second only to the Anglo-Saxon, and in
Saskatchewan and Alberta, where it ranks third.

There were in Canada in 1941, according to the census of that year,
305,929 persons of Ukrainian stock. However, Ukrainian was given as the
mother tongue by 313,273. Ukrainians themselves insist that these are
underestimates, and that there are in addition a large number of persons

of Ukrainian descent incorrectly recorded as Austrians, Poles, Rumanians or Hungarians. In any case the Ukrainian stock is numerically about equal to that of the Germans, whose census enumeration is 464,000, and is exceeded only by that of the Anglo-Saxons and French. It is much stronger than the Polish group (157,000) or the Russian (83,000). And politically it appears to be, under present circumstances, far more influential than the German group. In sharp contrast to the United States, where the Carpatho-Russian [Carpatho-Rusyn] community is roughly equivalent to the Ukrainian, there are in Canada very few Carpatho-Russians [Carpatho-Rusyns].

Fraternal insurance associations, which provide the framework of political functioning in the Ukrainian community of the United States, are very weak in Canada, and Ukrainian-Canadian views on foreign policy are expressed instead through cultural societies, chiefly of more or less Ukrainian nationalist viewpoint. During the between-wars period and at the time of the Nazi-Soviet pact, most of these societies worked steadily for Ukrainian independence. In 1941 under some official inspiration the nationalists, who are believed to make up 90 per cent of the community, consolidated their forces in a Ukrainian Canadian Committee. After the entrance of Russia into the war political efforts were completely subordinated to Canadian wartime necessities and to cultural work. Communist groups, always in a small minority, were suppressed by decree in June 1940, but are now, with the legal ban against Communists lifted, experiencing somewhat of a revival.

II. POLITICAL GROUPING

Although the politically active Ukrainian organizations in Canada are distinct from those in the United States, the general alignments on foreign policy are those traditional wherever Ukrainians are found. There are four chief groupings — an ultra-nationalist Right, represented in Europe by the Organization of Ukrainian Nationalists (OUN), a conservative monarchical Hetmanite movement, a Socialist sector, and a Communist-led Left.

Cutting across these political distinctions, the Ukrainian communities in America and Canada are divided along religious lines between a large Uniate Catholic group and a smaller Greek Orthodox, the latter split in turn between an autocephalous and an ecumenical branch.

Ukrainian National Federation: Ukrainian ultra-nationalism began to gain ground in Canada during the late 'twenties, finding support chiefly among younger immigrants who had arrived after the First World War. Founded in 1932, the Ukrainian National Federation *(Ukrainske Natsionalne Obyednannya — UNO)* was a counterpart of the Organization for the

Rebirth of the Ukraine *(ODWU)* organized at about the same time in the United States. Both looked for leadership to the European *OUN* (Organization of Ukrainian Nationalists). Although the *ODWU* became dormant after the outbreak of the war, the Canadian *UNO* continued to exist, and became the leading Ukrainian nationalist organization in Canada. The leader of the group is Professor Vladimir Kossar of the University of Saskatchewan, and its press organ the Winnipeg semi-weekly *Novy Shliakh* (New Pathway). Founded in 1930, published by the Ukrainian National Publishing Company, and having a circulation of 4,000, *Novy Shliakh* is edited by M. Pohorecky. Another important figure in the *UNO* is Professor T. K. Pavlichenko of the University of Saskatchewan.

Like the *ODWU* in the United States, the Canadian *UNO* looked to Hitler as the means through which Ukrainian independence or at least autonomy might be achieved, but after Hungary was allowed to seize the Carpatho-Ukraine, the *UNO's* mouthpiece, the *Novy Shliakh*, dropped its praise of the Nazi leader. It still, however, preaches a Ukrainian nationalism strongly tinged with totalitarian concepts.

The *UNO* was considerably strengthened by the confiscation of Communist properties early in the war. It was able to buy a number of former Communist-controlled community halls cheaply, and apparently also took over the Communist printing presses.

Restricted in political activities by the war, the *UNO* has turned to cultural enterprises, establishing summer courses to which lecturers from the United States have been invited. Late in March it was reported that a Ukrainian Educational Center had been formed under *UNO* auspices, with its headquarters at Winnipeg. It intends to conduct a student home and special educational courses, publish popular scientific books, and found a Ukrainian library and a museum. The executive board of the Center consists of Kossar, Pavlichenko, H. Hultay, Dr. P. Macenko, O. Tarnovetsky, Honore Ewach, and P. Bozhok.

The Hetmanites: More conservative than the *OUN* is the Hetmanite movement, a monarchical group cherishing the traditions of Ukrainian independence which it enjoyed during the last year of World War I, when Hetman Paul Skoropadsky headed under German auspices a puppet revival of a medieval Ukrainian kingdom. Skoropadsky, according to last reports, was living in the Berlin suburb of Wannsee as a protege of Goering. His son Danilo visited the United States and Canada before the war, and, in an itinerary arranged by Ukrainian Catholic leaders, including Bishop Vasyl Ladyka of the Uniate Catholic Church in Canada, visited Ukrainian-speaking communities as the representative of his father. He is now in England.

The Hetmanite movement was active in the United States until the outbreak of the war. It was then formally dissolved, but its anti-Soviet aims are now being promoted in renewed vigor by the Philadelphia tri-weekly *Ameryka* under its present editor, Bohdan Katamay. The factions supporting the *OUN* and Hetmanite views are united now in the Ukrainian Congress Committee.

In Canada the Hetmanite group was until 1939 organized in the Union of Hetman Organizations. The Hetmanites had a certain following among the Uniate Catholic clergy. The Hetmanite organization in Canada is very small. Officially disbanded in 1939, the group is still moderately active. Its organ is the weekly *Ukrainski Robitnyk* (Ukrainian Toiler) of Toronto, founded in 1935, with a claimed circulation of 5,600. It is edited by Michael Hethman and published by the Ukrainian Toiler Publishing Company. At one time, the Hetmanites also enjoyed the support of the weekly *Kanadiski Farmer* (Canadian Farmer). In 1930 Michael Hethman succeeded Vladimir Bossy as Hetmanite leader.

Brotherhood of Ukrainian Catholics: Although a section of the Ukrainian clergy supported the Hetmanite movement, the Catholics as a whole did not evince any great political activity until the outbreak of the war, when the Brotherhood of Ukrainian Catholics *(Bratstvo Ukraintsiv Katolykiv — BUK)* was organized under the leadership of the energetic Reverend W. Kushnir, whose election as president of the Ukrainian Canadian Committee, formed in 1943 largely through his efforts, gave prominence to the *BUK*. The *BUK* controls the 8-page weekly *Ukrainski Visty* (Ukrainian News) of Edmonton, Alberta, edited by John Esaiw, and claiming a circulation of 5,500. It also issues a weekly bulletin, the *Buduchnist Natsii* (Future of the Nation) published in Winnipeg. The monthly *Svitlo* (Light) published in Mundare, Alberta, by the St. Basil Order, is an allied journal.

Self-Reliance League: Representing the Ukrainian independence movement once headed in Europe by Simon Petliura, the Ukrainian Self-Reliance League *(Soyuz Ukraintsiv Samostiynykiv — SUS)* was founded in 1927. The largest, and at one time the most influential Ukrainian organization in Canada, it was in organization and program very similar to the now defunct Nationalist Defence of the Ukraine society in the United States. Moderately nationalist, *SUS* is traditionally hostile to the totalitarian *UNO* and to the Catholic monarchist *BUK*. It draws its chief strength from the Greek Orthodox congregations, and has organized a number of auxiliaries, including the Union of Ukrainian Community Centers *(Soyuz Ukrainskykh Domiv)*, the Canadian Ukrainian Youth Association *(Soyuz Ukrainskoi Molodi Kanady — SUMK)*, and the Ukrainian Women's Association *(Soyuz Ukrainok Kanady — SUK)*. Two educational institutions, the Mohyla Institute in Saskatoon, founded in 1916, and the Hrushevsky Institute in Edmonton, opened in 1919 — both connected with the Orthodox Church — are allied to the *SUS*. Its organ is the 12-page weekly *Ukrainski Holos* (Ukrainian Voice) of Winnipeg, founded in 1910, and published by the Ukrainian Publishing Company of Canada. The paper is edited by Miroslav Stechishin, since 1935 the leader of the group having then replaced Swystun who went over to the *UNO*. In March the *Ukrainski Holos* considered as a clear case of new appeasement Prime Minister Churchill's statement in his speech of 22 February that the British view on the matter of the Polish-Russian border is expressed in the Curzon Line.

The Socialists: The Socialist organizations in Canada although the first on the scene there, are now in a state of almost complete disorganization. The once strong Federation of Ukrainian Socialists, later the Ukrainian Social-Democratic Party, organized before the First World War, disbanded following a split with the Communists. Most of the present Socialist societies are of a local or regional character, without a national center. Among them are the Defense of the Ukraine organization with chapters in Toronto, Chatham (Ontario), and Montreal, which is connected with the organization of the same name in the United States; local groups in Toronto and elsewhere in the East with Social Revolutionary traditions; and a former Communist opposition group which left the Party in the early 'thirties and now has contacts with the Socialists. With a small following this last group has as leader Daniel Lobay, former editor of the Communist paper in Winnipeg, and now in charge of the group's organ in Toronto originally the *Dzvin* (Bell), later renamed the *Vpered* (Forward).

In the eastern part of Canada are a number of branches of the Socialist-line Ukrainian Workingmen's Association of Scranton, Pennsylvania.

The Communists: In the United States pro-Communist organizations have been fairly free to organize and carry on propaganda, and have consequently undergone little alteration; in Canada, however, the Communist Party was suppressed in 1940, and the pro-Communist Ukrainian organizations were dispersed in the same year. With the ban recently lifted, the Ukrainian-Canadian pro-Communists are vigorously attempting to revive their older organizations and appealing for support to the general Ukrainian-Canadian community.

The Ukrainian wing of the Canadian Communist Party was organized in 1918 by a group of left-wing Social Democrats, but operated chiefly through an ostensibly non-political organization known as the Ukrainian Labor-Farmer Temple Association (ULFTA), which at its height controlled over 100 local community halls, in which varied activities were carried on, including schools, courses, lectures, libraries, and dramatic and musical functions. The Communist organ, the *Narodna Hazeta* (People's Gazette), was the only Ukrainian-language daily. This activity was brought to a sudden halt 5 June 1940 when the Canadian Government banned the ULFTA, closed its halls, stopped the paper, and interned 36 of the leaders. Toward the end of 1941, some months after the German attack upon the Soviet Union, the Communist movement reemerged as the Ukrainian Association for Aid to the Fatherland, whose professed aim was the collection of funds for the benefit of the Soviet Union. At a convention in Winnipeg in June 1942 the name of the Association was changed to that of Ukrainian Canadian Association. When the ban against Communist organizations was recently lifted, the Association's leaders were released, and the group resumed its political activity. It has not yet, however, regained its earlier influence. The Association claims 10,000 members in 230 branches.

There are now two Communist-line weeklies, the *Ukrainske Zhittya* (Ukrainian Life) published in Toronto by the Canadian-Ukrainian Publishing Company, and the *Ukrainske Slovo* (Ukrainian Word), issued by the Ukrainian Word Publishing Company in Winnipeg.

At the time of the Ukrainian Canadian Congress in Winnipeg in June 1943, the Association directed bitter attacks against the Congress and its sponsor, the Ukrainian Canadian Committee, which it declared was fascist. The Association's chief activity in recent months has been aimed with some success at securing the return of the ULFTA halls. A recent appeal by the *Ukrainske Zhittya* to all Ukrainian organizations to unite, irrespective of their platforms, for the purpose of according joint aid to the Ukrainian cause has met with a charge by the Self-Reliance League's organ *Ukrainski Holos* that this is merely a new effort on the part of Moscow to silence critics of Soviet policy in democratic countries.

III. BACKGROUNDS

Two factors secure for the Ukrainian-Canadian group a much stronger position than their numbers would indicate. Their birth rate is relatively high, and they own huge areas of land.

Strength of Community: The birth rate of the Ukrainians is higher than that of the Anglo-Saxons and most other groups in Canada. In comparing the official statistics for 1941 with those of 1931, one notes decreases among Germans, Jews, Russians, Finns, Austrians, and Rumanians, while Ukrainians show about a 35 per cent increase, though in part this increase is probably also due to more accurate census methods.

Ukrainian immigrants to Canada, like those to the United States, came chiefly from Galicia, Bukovina, and Carpatho-Ukraine, although the relative representation of these regions varies in the two countries.

While immigrants from the barren mountain country of the Lemko region and the Carpatho-Ukraine are numerous in the United States, it was the inhabitants of the fertile Black Earth districts of Eastern Galicia (Podolia) and Bukovina who were attracted to the farmlands in Canada. Aside from this difference, both groups consist of the same stock, representing often the same counties, villages, and even families.

Most Ukrainians came to the United States to earn money with the intention of returning to the old country and improving their lot there. They turned to large industrial centres, and when the First World War made their return impossible, they remained here in the cities as workers or small businessmen. Canada, on the other hand, was the goal of those who sought land upon which to settle permanently. They sold their property in the old country and brought their families with them, determined to establish a new life for themselves in the North. Thus, in the United States, only a small fraction of the Ukrainian immigration lives on the land, whereas in Canada 80 per cent inhabit rural areas.

The area of Ukrainian land holdings has increased markedly since the First World War. During the period between the war and the depression of 1929 Ukrainian colonies spread steadily.

Extensive Settlements: Ukrainian immigrants colonized large sections of the three Western provinces of Manitoba, Alberta, and Saskatchewan, settling close together. Their rural settlements now extend from Southeastern Manitoba northward to a point east of Winnipeg, and thence along the Canadian National Railway as far west as Edmonton, Alberta. There are vast stretches of territory settled almost entirely by Ukrainians, and Ukrainians can be found in nearly every municipality in Northern Manitoba constituting a majority in most of them. In recent times, Ukrainian settlements have grown up in the Eastern provinces of Ontario and Quebec, as well as in British Columbia in the Far West.

Of the 20 per cent of Ukrainian Canadians living in cities throughout the Dominion [1931 Census], there are large groups in Winnipeg (25,000), Montreal (12,000), Toronto (10,000), Edmonton, Fort William, Hamilton, Saskatoon, Vancouver, and other cities. Large numbers of persons of Ukrainian stock are to be found in all mining districts throughout Canada. In lesser numbers they have found their occupations at railway centers, in lumber camps and saw mills.

Degree of Assimilation: The territorial compactness of Ukrainian settlements and the still preponderant proportion of first generation immigrants has greatly retarded assimilation. Although assimilation is rapid in the larger centers, there are great numbers of Ukrainian Canadians who live in villages which bear Ukrainian names, and who employ Ukrainian when dealing with banks, stores, etc. Some, in fact, rarely have occasion to hear the English language. Assimilation has on the whole been much slower than in the United States. In both countries there is a strong tendency for the second, and to a larger degree the third, generation to abandon the Ukrainian language, but in Canada the process is definitely less rapid and meets with greater resistance on the part of parents, who like to quote the late Governor-General Lord Tweedsmuir's dictum uttered before a Ukrainian gathering: "You will be better Canadians by being good Ukrainians."

Peasant Conservatism: Because of their descent from sturdy peasant stock and their preservation in Canada of a rustic existence, most Ukrainian-Canadians are more conservative than their brothers in America, and have preserved many of those qualities which are common to all peasants. Even the same political ideas and movements express themselves there in a more conservative form.

With the exception of the rural clergy and school teachers, the intellectual elements necessary for productive cultural life were not attracted to Canada by the hard physical conditions of life there, and, as a result, manifestations of cultural life have remained rudimentary. The press, as noted below, is of poor quality, put out mostly by non-professionals. Ukrainian literary productions are few and inferior. Personalities capable of playing a part in Canadian public life have been rare, although Ukrainians complain that there has been no scarcity of dishonest charlatans.

The Uniate and Orthodox Faiths: For Ukrainians in Canada, as in the United States, organizational activity began with the Church. The same three major Ukrainian religious groups exist in both countries. In Canada the Uniate Catholic group has its own bishop in the person of Vasyl Ladyka, who is assisted by a newly consecrated auxiliary bishop, Nil Savarin. There are two Greek Orthodox bodies, an autocephalous and an ecumenical, both subordinated to bishops in the United States. Archbishop John Theodorovitch of Philadelphia heads the former, Bishop Bohdan Shpylka of New York the latter. In Eastern Canada there are a few Ukrainian Protestant congregations of which the most important is the Russian-Ukrainian Baptist.

About two-thirds of the Ukrainian-Canadians are Uniate Catholics, while the remaining one-third are divided between the two Orthodox churches. As in the United States, the Uniate Catholic group is in general more conservative and politically inactive, but exercises strict control over its followers through its more rigid organization. It is also by far the wealthier.

Educational Institutions: Until 1916 there were bi-lingual schools in Manitoba and one in Regina, Saskatchewan, and in the latter province the Ukrainian language was taught in public schools. During the First World War, however, these bi-lingual schools were curtailed and finally discontinued. Teaching in the Ukrainian language is now conducted privately by local communities as a supplement to the official education. Evening courses in the Ukrainian language maintained by the regular teachers in the public school buildings are often regarded as official instruction even by non-Ukrainians.

There are several Ukrainian institutions devoted to secondary and higher education. Two institutes, the Mohyla Institute in Saskatoon (founded 1916) and the Hrushevsky Institute in Edmonton (founded 1919), are connected with the autocephalous Orthodox Church. The Uniate Catholics also maintain a very small institute in Edmonton. Courses in Ukrainian language and literature are taught at the University of Saskatchewan.

Social and Fraternal Organizations: The social organizations first assumed the form of reading halls and clubs, besides choral and dramatic groups. Canada has many Ukrainian civic centers, not only in the cities and towns, but also in the rural districts of Western Canada. In many localities there are Enlightenment (Prosvita) and other reading clubs, frequently named after the Ukrainian national poet Taras Shevchenko.

The benevolent associations, which in the United States form the basis of all organized life among Ukrainians and other Slavic groups, have been neglected in Canada. There are only smaller groups of this type, such as the Ukrainian Fraternal Society of Canada *(Ukrainske Tovarystvo Vzayemnoi Pomochi v Kanadi)* with quarters in Winnipeg. In recent times two American organizations, the Ukrainian National Association and the Ukrainian Workingmen's Association, have gained a foothold among Ukrainian-Canadians.

The Press: It was in the neighborhood of Winnipeg, Manitoba, that the first Ukrainian immigrant colonies were founded, and it was at Winnipeg that the first Ukrainian societies and the first Ukrainian-language newspapers appeared. In time Winnipeg became the headquarters of all the important Dominion-wide organizations.

The Ukrainian-language press in Canada is by no means as strong as the large Ukrainian-speaking population would appear to warrant. The papers are of a poor quality, produced chiefly by non-professional journalists. There are no dailies, only 1 semi-weekly, 7 weeklies, and, with monthlies and others, a total of 14 magazines and newspapers. The papers which serve as organs of political organizations or groups that were described above. The only important independent is the weekly *Kanadiski Farmer* (Canadian Farmer) which is also the oldest Ukrainian-language paper in Canada. Founded in Winnipeg in 1903 by F. Doyacek, a businessman of Czech origin who still publishes newspapers for various language groups, it was for a time, under the editorship of Theodore Dackiw, a Hetmanite organ. Dackiw, however, was discharged at the beginning of the war, and the *Kanadiski Farmer*, with Dr. K. Andrusyshyn as editor, is now independent. It is still published by Doyacek's National Publishers, and claims a circulation of 1,600.

The second paper to appear (1904) was the Winnipeg *Slovo* (Word), financed by the Conservative Party in opposition to the *Kanadiski Farmer,* at that time a Liberal Party organ; the *Slovo* has long since disappeared.

The first paper to be published by Ukrainians themselves was the Socialist weekly *Chervoni Prapor* (Red Banner) published in Winnipeg in 1907-08. In 1909 another Ukrainian Socialist newspaper, the *Robochi Narod* (Working People) began to appear in Winnipeg but was discontinued in 1918 by a Government decree affecting all Ukrainian and Socialist papers.

Early in the present century a number of religious journals were founded, one of which, *Ranok* (Morning) founded in 1904 still appears as a bi-weekly under the name of *Kanadiski Ranok* (Canadian Morning); it is published by the United Church of Canada and edited by the Reverend J. A. Cormie. Claimed circulation is 4,000.

In Canadian Politics: For a long time Ukrainian-Canadians kept aloof from Canadian political life, holding the view that all official and administrative matters fell within the domain of the Anglo-Saxons. As a result, Ukrainian-Canadians were not interested in representation in provincial legislatures or in the Dominion Parliament. Only in recent years has a change taken palce.

At present, Ukrainian-Canadians are strongly represented in municipal and local administration. There is only one representative in Ottawa — Anthony Hlynka, M.P. of the Social Credit Party, Vegreville, Alberta. There are seven representatives in the Manitoba legislature, and a few in those of Alberta and Saskatchewan.

In World War I: Ukrainian-Canadians are still under a handicap resulting from their experiences in the First World War. In 1914, immediately after the Austrian declaration of war upon Serbia, Ukrainian Catholic Bishop Budka of Winnipeg published a pastoral epistle calling upon Ukrainians to come to the defense of Austria. This letter was published on 27 July 1914, and although on 2 August [8 August] 1914, following the British declaration of war on Germany, Budka published another epistle in which he called upon Ukrainians to defend Canada and Great Britain, the first epistle had placed Ukrainian-Canadians in an unfavorable light. After the declaration of war some 3,000 Ukrainians held a public meeting and unanimously adopted a resolution pledging loyalty to the British flag and "readiness to rise in its defense, if necessary." Nevertheless, in 1916 the teaching of the Ukrainian language in the public schools was discontinued. In 1917, Ukrainians, along with other enemy aliens, lost the right to vote, and at the close of September 1918, the Government suspended the publication of Ukrainian papers. A month later, publication was permitted in two languages, Ukrainian and English, and the decree was revoked in April 1919.

Between the Wars: Following the war the Ukrainian-Canadians worked steadily for the cause of Ukrainian independence. In 1919 they sent to the Peace Conference in Paris a delegation consisting of John Petrushevich and O. Megas; its function was to co-operate with the main Ukrainian delegation at the Conference. In 1922 a delegation from the Ukrainian National Association of Eastern Canada called upon Prime Minister Mackenzie King to demand independence for Eastern Galicia, then under Polish rule. Winnipeg Ukrainians organized a great demonstration of 10,000 people to protest Polish atrocities against the Ukrainian people in Eastern Galicia. The Ukrainian Central Committee with headquarters in Winnipeg also sent to Mackenzie King a delegation from various provinces, and at that time the Prime Minister was given a memorial regarding the situation in Galicia. On 8 May 1931, the question of Polish pacification of Eastern Galicia was raised in the Dominion Parliament at Ottawa by Michael Luchkovich of Vegreville, Alberta. Prime Minister Bennett and ten representatives of various parties took part in the ensuing discussion.

IV. ACTIVITIES DURING WORLD WAR II

In the present war Canadian patriotism is stressed by Ukrainian-Canadians upon every possible occasion. According to their own estimates, Ukrainians have given Canada's armed forces up to fifty thousand volunteers. Great pride is taken in a statement made at the Ukrainian Canadian Congress by Lieutenant-Governor R. F. McWilliams who told the delegates: "Your record is one of the finest in this country, your contributions are not excelled by those of any Anglo-Saxons." Since this statement was made in the course of a speech in promotion of bond-buying, it should be discounted to some extent, and it is reported that the Ukrainian-Canadians have in fact not been buying bonds in proportion to their capacity.

When recently the Ukrainian-American *Svoboda* touched upon the possibility of a closer political tie between Canada and the United States, Ukrainian-Canadians generally repudiated the suggestion, the Catholic *Buduchnist Natsii* replying in its issue of 14 January: "We want to remain good neighbors, but we do not want to go too far. We are well off in Canada, and in many respects perhaps even better off than you are in America."

The Impact of Soviet Victories: In Canada, as in the United States and Latin America, the impending victory of the United Nations, and particularly the Soviet successes in Eastern Europe, have forced upon Ukrainian leaders a sharp re-evaluation of the foreign political scene. In the United States the chief results have been the revival of a united anti-Soviet front of both *OUN* and Hetmanite traditions in the Ukrainian Congress Committee, and the split of the Socialists between a pro-Soviet majority and an anti-Soviet minority. In Latin America the Hetmanites have created a Committee of Argentine Ukrainians with an ambitious program for a continent-wide union of anti-Soviet forces. In Canada the Ukrainian nationalists of all stripes except the pro-Soviet had organized during the period of the Nazi-Soviet pact in 1941 at Government initiative a Ukrainian Canadian Committee.

Consolidation in the Committee was preceded by a year-long rivalry between two committees set up early in 1940, one representing the Orthodox Self-Reliance League and the Hetmanites, the other the Catholic *BUK* and the nationalist *UNO*. The press dispute between the two groups became so bitter that the organ of the Self-Reliance League, the *Ukrainski Holos*, charged that the *UNO* was "executing the will of Berlin." Two days after this charge appeared both committees announced their consolidation as the Ukrainian Canadian Committee *(KUK)*.

This surprising turn in events was attributed by Ukrainians in Canada and the United States to the intervention of Dr. Tracy Philipps, a former British diplomat then in the Canadian service, who is said to have persuaded the two groups to a truce upon orders from his Government. Another influential person whose efforts helped to bring about the merger was Professor Watson Kirkconnell of McMaster University, reputed to be closely connected with Polish officialdom. Following the establishment of the Ukrainian Canadian Committee all ideological quarrels in Canada ceased.

The Ukrainian Canadian Congress: The outstanding wartime event of Ukrainian-Canadian political life was the Ukrainian Canadian Congress in Winnipeg 22-24 June 1943. Sponsored by the Ukrainian Canadian Committee consisting of the *BUK,* the Self-Reliance League, the *UNO,* the Hetmanites, and a small labor group of former Communist oppositionists, it was proclaimed by its sponsors as a successful unification of all political groups with the exception of the Communists and some small Socialist groupings. Over 600 delegates participated, and the Committee claimed the recognition of 1,429 organizations representing eighty per cent of the Ukrainian Canadians.

Since the Committee had adopted a sharp anti-Soviet stand and strongly advocated Ukrainian separatism, the Congress of 1943 was generally expected to adopt resolutions in the same spirit. The resolutions, however, avoided all mention of Ukrainian independence and were limited to general demands for "equal treatment of Ukrainians with the other recognized nations as a free and united member in the family of European nations."

"Nowhere in them [the resolutions]," noted the Jersey City *Svoboda's* English-language supplement 10 July, "is there the slightest direct mention of the fact that democratically-minded Ukrainians in their native land Ukraine and their kinsmen in Canada as well as here in America and elsewhere desire to see established after this war a free and independent state of Ukraine."

Professor Kirkconnell advised Ukrainians to reconcile themselves with the Poles. Representatives of several leading Polish organizations appeared at the Congress and delivered a memorandum appealing for an understanding between Poles and Ukrainians. While the memorandum was read, it was not applauded, nor was it referred to during the subsequent discussions. In general, topics discussed by the speakers dealt with Canadian affairs.

To Ukrainian Americans it appeared still more significant that the permanent Ukrainian Congress Committee appointed at the Congress, contrary to expectation, abandoned the political campaign for Ukrainian independence, and in addition to efforts on behalf of Canadian war activities, restricted itself to such cultural work as the publication of Ukrainian primers and other school books. This evasion of political questions by the Ukrainian Canadian Committee is also explained as due to official advice from Ottawa. The Canadian Government, it is said, has since been embarrassed by rumors, circulated by the Committee, that Ottawa had a hand in the formation of the Committee. These rumors may also provide a clue to recent public scoldings of the Committee delivered by Michael Hrechukha, head of the Ukrainian Soviet Socialist Republic, and by other persons in the Soviet Ukraine.

The Canadian Government is now reported to have reverted to a hands-off policy, and the Ukrainian Canadian Committee has become dormant.

Reaction to Soviet Decentralization: The announcement of Soviet constitutional changes met with divided opinions in the Ukrainian-Canadian press. While the organ of the Self-Reliance League, the *Ukrainski Holos* of Winnipeg, was critical, the independent *Kanadiski Farmer* commented favorably upon the event. In its issue of 9 February the *Ukrainski Holos* expressed doubt about the significance of the constitutional changes, voicing the nationalist and therefore the majority opinion in Canada:

> This is not a full measure of rights for each people. How about the finances? How about the schools? What about the various realms of economy? It will not make Ukrainians happy if they have an army in Archangelsk or Kamtchatka. It would not make Ukrainians happy if in

Ottawa the Ukraine were represented by a Postishev or a Rasputin appointed by Moscow, and if Khrushchov were appointed dictator of the Ukraine.

The other view, expressed by the *Kanadiski Farmer* of 8 February, regards the changes "an important turning point having great, albeit unforeseen, repercussions upon the structure of the postwar world." In its 16 February editorial, the same paper said:

We concede that the Ukrainian Republic is not entirely independent and that it depends upon the supreme leadership of the Soviet Union. This is correct. But what sort of independence can European people expect from a victorious Germany?

Poland and the Ukraine: Ukrainian-Canadian newspapers of all colors have joined during recent months in attacking Polish claims to Ukrainian territory. The Polish Government-in-Exile, said the Self-Reliance League's *Ukrainski Holos*, had lost its opportunity to accept Soviet terms without losing face, and had no choice but to capitulate. Poland, it suggested, might soon become the seventeenth Soviet Republic. Neither a Russian-Ukrainian nor a Polish-Ukrainian understanding was possible as long as both Russians and Poles maintained a superior attitude toward Ukrainians, declared the same paper in a later issue. Ukrainians would like friendship with both neighbors, but would refuse to have them as guardians; Ukrainian-Canadians had no right to "choose protectors" for their European compatriots.

"All Ukrainians, and in this case the western Ukrainians are no exception," said the *UNO's Novy Shliakh*, "crave Ukrainian national independence and no servitude, be it Polish or Russian." The independent *Kanadiski Farmer* denied that Poland had a right to Ukrainian territories, in which, it said, the Poles were an insignificant minority; Poland should be restored after the war within its ethnographic borders, and if the Polish Government accepted this solution, it would save itself and the Polish people much trouble. The *BUK's Ukrainski Visty* asserted that all the current press comment on the "Curzon Line" was inaccurate, since the line was originally drawn before the Polish-Soviet war as a provisional boundary between Poland and the Western Ukrainian Republic. The line, the Communist-line *Ukrainske Zhittya* pointed out, did not take in the Ukrainian provinces of Kholm and Lemko, nor parts of Polissya and Eastern Galicia. The present plight of the Polish Government-in-Exile, said the Hetmanite *Ukrainski Robitnyk*, is just punishment for past Polish sins towards Poland's neighbors. It described as predatory and imperialistic Poland's past policy with respect to Galicia, Czechoslovakia, and Lithuania, and said that the Polish claim that Great Britain had guaranteed

Poland's territorial integrity was totally unfounded, since Britain's guarantee in 1939 had referred only to Poland's independence.

Germany, Poland, or Russia?: With their dream of an anti-Communist independent Ukraine shattered, the Ukrainian nationalists are deeply torn in their sympathies among the three neighboring powers — Germany, Poland, and Russia. Many Ukrainian Canadians, it is reliably reported, would still prefer German control over the Ukraine to that of either Soviet Russia or Poland, but with the impending defeat of Germany they are left with a choice between Poland and Russia. Their strongest feeling, it is said, is hatred for the Poles — even to the point of preferring to see the Ukraine under the domination of Soviet Russia with religion suppressed rather than ruled by a "capitalistic Poland."

Ukrainian War Relief: In Canada as in the United States the Ukrainian community has been split on the question of war relief to Ukrainians, the pro-Communists being at least in part interested in such relief as a means of aiding the Soviet Union, while Ukrainian nationalists are suspicious of aid transmitted through Soviet agencies. Since aid is now possible only through Soviet agencies, the pro-Communist groups have been considerably more active in relief campaigns. Typical was a mass meeting held in Toronto 20 May under the auspices of the pro-Communist Ukrainian-Canadian Association for the purpose of raising funds to equip a hospital now at Lwow [Lviv] in Galicia and one at Cernauti [Chernivtsi] in Bukovina. The general goal of the Association's drive is $50,000, of which $10,085 was contributed at the Toronto meeting. Chairman of the meeting was P. Prokopchak, an Association official, and the three principal speakers were Ivan Boychuk, the leading Ukrainian-Canadian Communist figure; Ivan I. Volenko, Third Secretary of the Soviet Legation; and Lieutenant Colonel E. Timchenko, a member of the staff of the Soviet Commercial Attache in Ottawa. The only reference to the question of Ukrainian independence was a brief statement by Volenko on the development of the Ukraine under Soviet rule and the devastation suffered from German occupation, with a declaration that the struggle of the Ukraine for liberation and national integrity could be successful only within the framework of the Soviet Union. Telegrams of greeting were exchanged with the Ukrainian Soviet Socialist Republic, along with a pledge by the meeting of support for the Ukrainian people. The formal occasion for the meeting was the anniversary of the Ukrainian poet, Ivan Franko.

A similar meeting was held 11 June in Winnipeg, at which over $7,000 was collected for the two hospitals. The liberation of the Ukraine from the invader furnished the theme. Volenko was again among the guests present; others were Chief Justice McPherson, Acting Premier of Manitoba, and a Colonel Jones who represented the Canadian armed forces. There was a street parade with national costumes and banners containing slogans of greeting to the Red Army.

Representing the opposing nationalist view on relief, the *UNO* organ *Novy Shliakh* in editorials 14 and 17 June criticized severely articles in the Jersey City *Svoboda* urging the necessity of immediate relief regardless of the possibility that distribution would have to be largely through Soviet agencies. "One American nationalist paper," said the *Novy Shliakh*, "recently raised the question [of relief] in a rather infelicitous and vague manner. This step was exploited by the Bolsheviks in their campaign 'to aid the Ukraine.' We regard this step by the American paper as precipitate and ill-considered." Ukrainians should not be advised, *Novy Shliakh* cautioned, to believe that contributions to the "Communists" would reach "our poor people."

SOURCE: National Archives of the United States, RG 226, Entry 100, Box 119, 7N-B-Int-33

Ukrainian-Canadian soldiers serving on the Continent were the first to encounter Ukrainian Displaced Persons (DPs), as early as the summer of 1944. Utilizing their London-based Ukrainian Canadian Servicemen's Association (UCSA) they formed the Central Ukrainian Relief Bureau (CURB) to help these political refugees. Financially they were supported by the Ukrainian Canadian Committee's Ukrainian Canadian Relief Fund (UCRF). These Ukrainian-Canadian relief and resettlement efforts continued until 1951. However, the initial effort to create such a Fund was not accepted with equanimity by the government which feared adverse international repercussions.

No. 40: Confidential Letter from N. Robertson, Under-Secretary of State for External Affairs, to G. Pifher, Director of Voluntary and Auxiliary Services, Department of National War Services, November 15, 1944, Concerning Application of the Ukrainian Canadian Committee to Establish a "Canadian Ukrainian Refugee Fund"

CONFIDENTIAL

Ottawa, November 15, 1944

TO: George Pifher, Esq.
   Director of Voluntary and Auxiliary Services
   Department of National War Services
   Ottawa

I am writing in reply to your letter of October 30th, concerning the application of the Ukrainian-Canadian Committee to set up a "Canadian Ukrainian Refugee Fund" to aid Ukrainian refugees from Western Europe, North Africa and the Middle East.

2. While I agree that aid to displaced stateless persons can best be rendered by an international organization like the Red Cross, I think that it would be inadvisable to register the proposed Fund as a Red Cross auxiliary at the present time. It seems to me that the Committee are in error when they state on page four of their brief that persons from Western Ukraine would find themselves in the position of stateless and homeless refugees by virtue of the fact that their territory is in dispute between two powers. It would have been accurate so to describe their position if neither of the two powers concerned wished to accept them as citizens. There is no evidence at present that this is the case. It is quite probable that before the end of the war an agreement will be reached between the authorities concerned, which would allow these persons to opt freely for the citizenship of either state.

3. Under present political circumstances in Europe, the action of the Canadian Government in authorizing the Ukrainian Refugee Fund is likely to be misconstrued by both the Polish and the Soviet Governments. As you know, both Governments have accused certain Ukrainian groups in Europe of collaborating with the German Army in Poland and the Soviet Ukraine. There is some evidence to support these charges in the case of the Hetman Organization in Germany, and to a lesser extent in the case of Ukrainian Nationalists. The proposal of the Ukrainian Canadian Committee may well appear to the Polish and Soviet Governments as an attempt to rescue these Ukrainian collaborationists, especially since the Committee have been severely criticized by both Poles and Russians as representing, in so far as their aspirations for an independent Ukraine are concerned, the views of the Ukrainian groups which have allegedly assisted the Germans.

4. We are, of course, absolutely certain of the loyalty of the Ukrainian Canadian Committee to Canada. The support of its members for the war effort of this country has been excellent in every respect. I am afraid,

however, that in view of its international implications, a Canadian-Ukrainian Refugee Fund, operating under the auspices of the Committee, would prove to be a source of considerable ambarrassment to the Canadian Government.

5. I would suggest, therefore, that the Ukrainian Canadian Committee should be persuaded to abandon this project. It might be pointed out to them that by supporting the Canadian Red Cross they will be doing all that can be done at present to assist their compatriots abroad, since the Red Cross aids persons in distress regardless of their nationality. It would also be advisable to clarify their minds regarding the term "stateless refugees." I should not, however, on any account, mention to them the considerations in paragraphs three and four of this letter. These are stated here only for your own confidential information.

I should like to thank you for bringing this matter to my attention, and I should be grateful if you would continue to keep me informed of any further developments in this connection.

[sgd.] N. A. ROBERTSON
Under-Secretary of State
for External Affairs

SOURCE: Department of External Affairs
(Canada), History Section, File: 2514 - 40c

No. 41: Circular Letters No. 20 and No. 21 from the Ukrainian Canadian Servicemen's Association (Active Service Overseas), August 25 and September 30, 1945, Indicating UCSA's Participation in Ukrainian Relief Work and Appeal for Support

UKRAINIAN CANADIAN SERVICEMEN'S ASSOCIATION
(Active Service Overseas)
218 SUSSEX GARDENS, PADDINGTON, LONDON, W.2

CIRCULAR LETTER No. 20

August 25th, 1945

[........]

6. UKRAINIAN RELIEF COMMITTEE

With the return of our Servicemen to their respective homes the function of our Ukrainian centre in London will not completely end. The time

and effort of our executive members who will remain in this country for
some time will be occupied in a worthwhile manner with the problems and
welfare of our Ukrainian refugees. We cannot permit their urgent appeals
to go unanswered and for that reason every effort should be made to continue the support of our Ukrainian Club in London. A great deal of moral
and material help must be immediately forthcoming from all Ukrainians
who understand their plight, if their critical situation is to be alleviated. A
Ukrainian United Relief Committee has been formed to handle all their
problems. You may assist by compiling and sending in all information
pertaining to Ukrainian refugees. Such items as clothes, food, cigarettes
and money are urgently needed. Your contribution regardless of size or
nature will be greatly appreciated. All such help will be forwarded to the
proper Committee.

[........]

* * *

UKRAINIAN CANADIAN SERVICEMEN'S ASSOCIATION
(Active Service Overseas)
218 SUSSEX GARDENS, PADDINGTON, LONDON, W.2

CIRCULAR LETTER No. 21

September 30th 1945

[........]

4. CENTRAL UKRAINIAN RELIEF BUREAU

Under the joint auspices of the Ukrainian Canadian Relief Fund,
which is an Auxiliary of the Canadian Red Cross, and the United Ukrainian American Relief Committee, Incorporated, authorized by the President's War Relief Control Board, there has been opened in the same
building as our Club, a Central Relief Bureau. The purpose of the Bureau
in brief is to extend any and every moral and material aid possible on
behalf of the Sponsoring Committees, to all Ukrainian Refugees, Displaced Persons and destitute on the Continent.

The Bureau will work closely with U.N.R.R.A., Military Government, and all other official bodies responsible for Displaced Persons. We
would appeal to all our members, and particularly to those members who
are now on the Continent to send any information that they possibly can
obtain with regard to the locations, numbers and the moral, material and
physical conditions of Ukrainian refugees anywhere on the Continent. We
would also appeal to all our members to pass this information to anybody
to whom it might be of value and of interest. The Bureau office is a
separate office entirely removed from our Servicemen's organization, and

all correspondence relating to, or dealing with refugee or relief work should be addressed to:

Central Ukrainian Relief Bureau
218 Sussex Gardens, Paddington, London, W.2.

We would also ask all our members to inform their friends and relatives back in Canada about the formation of the Bureau and its purpose. It is estimated that there are still over one million Ukrainian refugees in the British and American zones who require assistance and relief, and it is the Social, Christian and Humanitarian duty of all of us to aid these countrymen.

[........]

SOURCE: Archives of Ontario,
G.R.B. Panchuk Collection

Senior bureaucrats felt that 'Old World' attachments would dissipate with the passage of time. They cautioned against overt interference in immigrant community affairs.

No. 42: Confidential Memorandum from L. Malania, Section Head (Soviet Desk), Department of External Affairs to H. Wrong, Associate Under-Secretary of State for External Affairs, December 5, 1945, Relaying his Conversation with M. Manuilsky, Commissar for the Soviet Ukrainian Foreign Affairs

[COPY[*CONFIDENTIAL*

**CANADIAN DELEGATION TO THE PREPARATORY
COMMISSION OF THE UNITED NATIONS**

BY BAG   14 Berkeley Street,
London W.1
5th December, 1945

Dear Mr. Wrong,

You will be interested in the report of a long conversation which I had with M. D.Z. Manuilsky, Commissar for Foreign Affairs of the Ukraine, who is the Ukrainian delegate to the Preparatory Commission. [........]

The subject M. Manuilsky was anxious to discuss was that of anti-Soviet Ukrainians in Canada. He began by saying many complimentary things about our country. [........]

M. Manuilsky then went on to say that sentiment aside, relations with Canada were of considerable practical value to the Soviet Union since there were really only two countries which could supply the U.S.S.R. with the materials necessary for reconstruction — the United States and Canada, "perhaps also the United Kingdom, though to a lesser extent." He felt that the question of credits would be solved in due course to the satisfaction of both countries. There was, however, one circumstance which marred Canadian-Soviet relations, and that was the anti-Soviet agitation conducted by certain groups of Ukrainians in Canada. It was difficult for Soviet-Ukrainians to reconcile, particularly after what they had gone through in the last few years, the licence allowed by the Canadian Government to anti-Soviet Ukrainians with the expressions of genuine friendship, of which there were many, and which he himself had witnessed when he passed through Edmonton last summer. M. Manuilsky stated at the outset that he understood and respected our principles of freedom of speech and right of asylum, but he felt that even these principles had certain bounds which should not be transgressed.

I told M. Manuilsky that Canadian officials were also seriously concerned about this problem, although from a different point of view. From the Canadian point of view it was not only a question of international relations, but a broader internal issue of Canadian nationality. The Canadian method of handling national minorities who had recently immigrated into the country differed from the nationality policies of the Soviet Union. We hoped that in due course this immigrant stock would be absorbed into one or the other of the two main ethnic groups in Canada.

This process took time. Every thoughtful Canadian understood that it was impossible for a man who came from another country to divest himself at one stroke of all the emotional associations of his early life. One could accuse him of moral dishonesty if he claimed to have done so. It was therefore perfectly natural for these immigrants to group themselves in societies which maintained the language and folk ways of their native land. Indeed, the Canadian authorities welcomed the existence of these societies since through their various activities they served to lessen the newcomer's sense of isolation in a new country. The second generation acquired naturally the ways of their adopted country and the third and fourth generations were thoroughly Canadian in outlook, but to the first generation of immigrants their native land would always remain a kind of sentimental and idealized symbol. This was especially true of the Ukrainians, most of whom had emigrated owing to circumstances which M. Manuilsky had doubtless known at first-hand. The educated element in this emigration, which provided the natural leadership for these societies, had been brought up in an atmosphere of intense Ukrainian nationalism. The ideal of an independent Ukraine continued to have for them a sentimental value, but the remarkable growth of the Soviet Union had deprived this ideal of all practical meaning.

What worried thoughtful Canadians was the exaggerated importance which was attached in the Soviet Union to this sentimental nationalism. Attacks in the Soviet press, such as Zaslavsky's articles, invested Ukrainian nationalist leaders with a significance which they would not otherwise have. I felt sure that M. Manuilsky's experience in handling problems of minority nationalism would support my contention that a minority national group tended to rally about any cause no matter how bad it might be if it felt that the attack on the cause was an attack upon itself. This had been the effect of Zalavsky's articles. Those Ukrainian Canadians who were pro-Soviet took their lead from articles in the Soviet press which attacked the nationalist organizations. This tended to rally the nationalists around their cause while their leaders felt that they were making headway when so powerfull a country as the U.S.S.R. took such vigorous notice of their activities.

From the Canadian point of view the effect of this controversy was to keep Ukrainian nationalism alive and thus to retard the process of assimilation. I suggested that the solution of this problem would be eased if the Ukrainian nationalists were ignored by the Soviet authorities while the Ukraine went on ahead with its programme of improving the life of the Ukrainian people.

I then asked M. Manuilsky on a purely personal and unofficial basis what concrete steps for solving this problem would he recommend to the Canadian Government if he were an official of that Government and had to take into account the constitutional framework within which it had to operate. M. Manuilsky evaded the issue by stating that if analogous statements were made about Canada in the Soviet Union, the Soviet authorities would deal very severely with the offenders. I said that if the Canadian Government attempted to use any form of repression, such as arrest, prohibition of the right to publish newspapers etc., the issue would become much greater than that of Ukrainian nationalism. The Canadian people would feel that their fundamental rights were threatened and would vigorously resist the Government's action. If any repressive action were taken because of anti-Soviet statements, then all the anti-Soviet elements in Canada would attempt to exploit popular attachment to civil liberties for their own ends and this would certainly have the worst possible effect on Canadian-Soviet relations. M. Manuilsky suggested that at least a strong statement on this subject by the Prime Minister might help to allay the uneasiness felt by the Soviet-Ukrainians. I wondered in reply whether such a statement might not give the anti-Soviet elements an opening for precipitating a public controversy over Soviet-Canadian relations in general. A statement of this sort might well defeat its own purpose.

I added that as a matter of fact the Canadian Government was studying this problem from the point of view of Canadian unity as well as of Soviet-Canadian relations, and that it seemed to me that the most effective policy under the present circumstances was to develop good all around Canadian-Soviet relations, in trade, exchanges of information, visits of scientists etc., and to avoid doing anything which might excite strong emotions. M. Manuilsky again asked me to give further thought to this problem with a view to formulating some more positive recommendations to the Government. He himself disclaimed, however, any right to give me any advice on how it should be handled.

I do not know whether I succeeded in convincing M. Manuilsky of the harmfulness of Soviet press attacks on Ukrainian nationalists, but I am glad that I had the opportunity of suggesting to him the complexity of the problem and of outlining the position of the Canadian Government. My impression is that he had not really considered the problem from this point of view, and that, as an old revolutionary, he had thought of it almost entirely in terms of polemical frontal assaults.

Lest my detailed account of the arguments should convey a false impression of acrimoniousness, I might add that the conversation, which was carried on in Russian, was conducted in an atmosphere of great cordiality, and even intimacy. [........]

H.H. Wrong Esq.   Yours sincerely,
Associate Under-Secretary
   of State for External Affairs   L. MALANIA
Ottawa, Canada

SOURCE: Department of External Affairs
(Canada), History Section, File: 165 - 39c

Speaking officially on behalf of the Canadian Government Stanley Knowles not only condemned Ukrainian-Canadian agitation against the Soviets but indicated that Canadian public opinion was also indisposed towards such political behaviour.

No. 43: Letter from L. Malania, Member of the Delegation for Canada, to the Secretary of State for External Affairs, December 22, 1945, Includes Transcript of the Exchange between S. Knowles, Canadian Delegate to the Preparatory Commission of the United Nations, and the Soviet Delegate, M. Manuilsky, December 15, 1945, Discussing the Issue of Refugees and Ukrainian Canadian Activities.

CANADIAN DELEGATION
to the
PREPARATORY COMMISSION OF THE UNITED STATES

CONFIDENTIAL

14, Berkeley Street
London W. 1

22 December 1945

Sir,

I have the honour to refer to my telegram No. 48 of December 17 regarding the discussion in Committee 1 on the subject of refugees. In that telegram I reported that M. Manuilsky, the Foreign Commissar of the Ukraine, made a direct reference to the anti-Soviet agitation of certain Ukrainians in Canada, and that Mr. Knowles made an excellent reply to M. Manuilsky.

I think you will be interested in seeing the verbatim report of this brief exchange and I accordingly enclose a copy of an extract from the minutes [.........].

I think you will agree that Mr. Knowles handled the situation admirably. His comment was sound and good humoured. I understand that the Soviet and Ukrainian delegates were greatly amused when Mr. Knowles referred to his own case as an illustration of the tolerance of the Canadian Government towards groups holding different opinions. I also

understand that the reply of Mr. Knowles has occasioned favorable
private comments among the other Delegations.

I have the honour to be,

Sir,

Your obedient servant,

[sgd.] L. MALANIA

for the Delegate for Canada

The Secretary of State for External Affairs
        Ottawa, Canada

P.S. I may add that no report of this exchange has appeared in any of the
local press.

*   *
*

**Seventeenth Meeting of Committee I, Preparatory Commission of the
United Nations, Church House, Saturday 15th December, 1945**

President: Mr. Colban

Delegate from Ukraine: Mr. President [........] my country attaches particular importance to the problem of refugees. I should like to address the
question clearly. There have been in the history of Europe very difficult
times for both political and religious refugees seeking refuge in certain
free countries. In those times everyone agreed, given that there existed
feudal and reactionary regimes, that it was necessary to give shelter and
protection to the refugees. But, I ask you, Mr. President, if it could be the
same today. Who are the present refugees? You yourself represent a country where a Quisling has played a role. This is not a phenomenon peculiar
to your country. There have been many other Quislings. And now, after
the fall of fascism, those elements which betrayed free nations could come
to pass themselves off as political refugees. I ask you, gentlemen, you who
represent the spirit of liberty, if we can now accept such a proposition
[........].

I shall emphasize the reasons why my country attaches such importance to this point. Ukraine has been invaded by the Germans. Since 1917
there had been elements in Ukraine which worked against their country
and, at the gravest of moments, when my country was fighting the Germans, these elements served our enemies. I represent a people which has

particularly suffered. I do not believe that the organization of the United Nations should occupy itself with the elements to which I have alluded. The honorable delegate from Canada is present here. I know that there is this sort of element in Canada. I address the Representation of Canada directly and say to him: Suppose that there were elements who criticized or even participated in certain acts directed against the United Nations. Are we going to protect them as refugees?

I demand that the proposition of the Economic and Social Council not be put on the agenda and I believe that it is by error that such a proposition has been made.

[........]

Delegate of Canada: [........] Mr. Chairman, one of the main reasons I was anxious to get to my feet before you put the closure motion was so that I might, with your indulgence, say a word or two in a very friendly way, but nonetheless definitely to my good friend Mr. Manuilsky, who in his remarks had occasion to refer to my country and to some of the things that go on in Canada. I want to say to him very sincerely that I am a little bit sorry that he made the comment, not because I take any offense, and I will tell him in a minute why I do not take any offense — or maybe I should tell him now. In our Parliament at home, I am a Socialist, sitting on the op-position side, opposed to the capitalist Government. So any criticism made of that Government does not offend me at all. I spend my days at home saying worse things about it than you might imagine. But the reason I am sorry the remark was made, and I was glad to see the Press were not present, and perhaps it would not travel home to Canada, is that when that kind of criticism is made, it simply incites the people who are doing the thing which my honorable friend and I both deplore, it incites them to do it all the more. I want to say that I personally, and in this instance I can speak for the Government I oppose, deplore the divisions amongst our Ukrainian people in Canada, and deplore the anti-Soviet utterances that are heard a good many times, many a time on the floor of our own House of Commons; when people have made such utterances, I have many times been among those shouting "shame" that such utterances were made. But we have a little different concept, perhaps, about our national life. We call it a certain form of Democracy, in which we give these people, the people within our country, the right to hold, and to express their opinions, even though we may deplore terribly the views they are expressing. And I give particular evidence of that concept of Democracy by the reference I have already made to my presence here. The Government in Canada, so-called Liberal Government, could have sent to this Conference a Delegation made up entirely of people supporting it. But they chose rather, and I give them the credit for it, to include in the Delegation persons like myself who

represent minority groups in the country, so all the views might find expression here.

It is in that structure of society, that kind of background, that statements are made sometimes that the majority of our people deplore. And I
hope this discussion between us will not get back there, because if it does,
it will just make the people saying the things my honorable friend deplores
feel they are heroes and carry on with it. But I can assure him, not only the
Government, but all responsible parties in Canada, do deplore very much
the things to which he referred tonight, and it is because there are these
conditions which require some satisfactory airing and satisfactory settling
that I feel it is important that this item should be on the agenda.

SOURCE: Department of External Affairs
(Canada), History Section, File: 8196 - 40c
[Translated from French]

---

*The character of postwar international relations required a
new form of intervention on the part of the Ukrainian Canadian
Committee. It responded with this appeal advocating* de jure
*recognition of the sovereign rights of the Ukrainian people to self-
determination. Critically, minimizing their own role to speak on
behalf of the Ukrainian nation, they pointed to the existence of
politically legitimate groups which they claimed represented the
true will of the Ukrainian people.*

*No. 44: Submission of the Ukrainian Canadian Committee to the
Paris Peace Conference, September 1946, Regarding the Political
Status of Ukraine*

MEMORANDUM
By
UKRAINIAN CANADIAN COMMITTEE
to
PARIS PEACE CONFERENCE
September, 1946

YOUR EXCELLENCIES:

On behalf of Canadians of Ukrainian origin who feel a deep concern for the fate of the Ukrainian people in Europe with whom they are bound by blood, culture, and tradition, the Ukrainian Canadian Committee regards its solemn duty to submit to your attention and careful consideration the following facts:

1. At the Peace Conference in Paris *Ukraine* is represented as a Ukrainian Soviet Socialist Republic by a man who is by no means its real and true representative, and has no authority from the Ukrainian nation, numbering some 45 million people, to speak on its behalf. The Ukrainians in the Ukraine did not elect or choose him as their representative. The so-called representative or representatives, as the case may be, is or are only appointees of the Russian Communist party acting through the Russian Politbureau. Therefore any statements made by such representatives at the Peace Conference or elsewhere are not the expression and the will of the Ukrainian nation but the will of Moscow.

This being so, it is obvious that *the Ukrainian people cannot take any responsibility for any opinions, tactical moves, falsehoods, provocations and motions of this so-called "Ukrainian Delegation,"* so much more so since this delegation attempts, and quite successfully does obstruct the achievement and bringing about of world peace at this time.

Furthermore, *the Ukrainian people could not consider themselves to be co-signatories to any decisions* at the Peace Conference and to be bound by them, especially those decisions pertaining to Ukrainian territories, population and its political future.

Consequently, we are not surprised that the Ukrainian people reserve for themselves the right and full freedom to fight such decisions with all means at their disposal, including even an open armed revolt. We state this quite frankly. From reliable sources, to which we have access, we learn that for that very reason a state of actual warfare exists at the present time all over the Ukraine, especially in the West, carried on by the Ukrainian Partisan Army, (UPA), which is operating against the Russian occupants in spite of all the attempts to crush this powerful movement.

2. We maintain that there exist authoritative Ukrainian groups in the Ukraine as well as outside of it, which without any doubt whatsoever, can be considered truly representative of the Ukrainian people and they are in position to really express the will of the Ukraine. They are:

(a) Ukrainian members of the last Parliament of the Polish Republic, elected on the basis of a general and a free franchise by secret ballot, including the vice-president of this Parliament, who now resides somewhere in western Europe in exile;

(b) Members of the former democratic Ukrainian Government, including several members of Parliament of the free Ukrainian Republic which existed up to the time of the Russian conquest in 1921, also living in exile;

(c) Finally, there exists a well organized Ukrainian partisan army in Ukraine, fighting against the oppression of the Soviet Regime and its armed forces. This army was instrumental in disrupting German communication and supply lines behind the Eastern (German-Soviet) front during the war. The existence and activities of this army were officially and repeatedly mentioned by the Soviet administration of Ukraine. Mr. Khrushchow, premier of the Soviet Government of the Ukraine; Mr. Manuilsky, head of the Department of Foreign Affairs of the Soviet Ukraine, as well as the Polish Minister of War, General Rolya Zymierski, not to mention the numerous correspondents of various American and British newspapers, all at one time or another mentioned that UPA has been very active and was fighting for the one and only cause — a sovereign Ukraine, free from Russian oppression and domination.

We propose that representatives of only such authoritative Ukrainian groups be admitted to the Peace Conference in a way and capacity similar to those in which in the year 1919 at the Versaille Conference were admitted the representatives of the Poles (Paderewsky), Czechoslovaks (Masaryk), Lithuanians, Latvians, Estonians and to a certain extent even the representatives from the Western Ukraine Government (Paneyko). [........]

So long as this true Ukrainian representation is not admitted to the Peace Conference and not heard by Your Excellencies, the *Ukrainian people all over the world cannot consider themselves properly and justly represented at the Conference,* and, therefore, will not consider themselves bound by its decisions.

3. Finally, we submit to the Peace Conference the general opinion of the Ukrainian people regardless of where they live, in the Ukraine, in exile as refugees, in the United States, in Canada, in South America and elsewhere, *that the whole scheme of aggression against the Ukrainian people in Ukraine and the establishment of a free and sovereign Ukrainian State be brought before the present Peace Conference and decided upon according to the terms of the Atlantic Charter, and the principles of self-determination and independence of every nation.*

[........]

4. From the *legal point* of view the Union of the Soviet Socialist Republics (Russia) has no rights of sovereignty or supremacy over the Ukraine. There is only one legal act in the past which bound for some time the Ukraine with Russia. This is the treaty of *Pereyaslav,* contracted on January 18, 1654, which established a *personal union* between Russia and

Ukraine in the person of the Tzar, leaving both countries mutually sovereign and independent.

This treaty of Pereyaslav has been constantly violated by Russia and finally broken completely in 1774, when the last stronghold of Ukrainian freedom, the Zaporogean Sitch, was incorporated by Empress Catherine II into Russia. Consequently, the said treaty became void, a legal tie between Russia and the Ukraine ceased to exist. Later the Ukraine was gradually conquered by a series of wars, and its democratic freedom-loving population enslaved.

Nevertheless, by accumulating forces and uniting them at proper occasions with other resisting forces inside of the Russian Empire (Polish, Finnish, Baltic, Caucasians, etc.), including Russia's own revolutionary movement, never did the Ukraine stop to resist the brutal conquerors. When, in 1917, the Russian Tzarist rule was overthrown, the Ukraine (Ukrainian Central Council) proclaimed its independence and became a Ukrainian National Republic. *This Ukrainian Republic was recognized de jure* by the new Russian (Communistic) government on December 4, 1917, by a decree of the Council of the People's Commissars, published in the official organ of the Russian government on December 6, 1917 (No. 25). Therefore, *Russia waived every right over the Ukraine by the same government which is ruling Russia at the present time.* Further expansion of Communism and military subjugation of the Ukraine by Russia (U.S.S.R.) did not change its legal status.

One should bear in mind that the Ukrainian Republic of 1917 was *de-facto* recognized by the government of Great Britain (January, 1918, appointment of Sir Picton Bagge as a representative) and by the government of France (December, 1917, appointment of Gen. Tabouis as a representative).

The Western part of the Ukraine (Galicia) was annexed by Russia in 1939 by the partition of Poland between U.S.S.R. and Hitlerite Germany. Again after a victory over Hitler, Bukovina and Carpatho-Ukraine, were annexed by Russia, although they never were part of Russia. The political status of these territories after the First World War was derived from the treaties of Versaille and St. Germain (1919). The status of East Galicia, according to these terms of self-determination, was still pending some decision of the League of Nations, which decision was never given before the outbreak of hositilities in 1939. *The annexation of all of these Ukrainian territories by the U.S.S.R. is an act of military conquest, which alone does not constitute legal rights to gain full possession and sovereignty over them.*

[........]

These facts and opinions our Committee presents for the consideration and attention of Your Excellencies in the belief that in this way it contributes its utmost to the cause of freedom, democracy and peace in the world.

SOURCE: Archives of Ontario,
G.R.B. Panchuk Collection

To strengthen their organizational structures in Canada community spokesman petitioned the government to admit Ukrainian Displaced Persons. Their appeals were based on the view that Canadian authorities wanted additional Ukrainian agricultural and unskilled labourers. They assumed that the government also wanted Ukrainian immigrants whom they characterized as being much like themselves.

No. 45: Memorandum from the Ukrainian Canadian Committee to the Rt. Hon. W. L. Mackenzie King, Prime Minister of Canada, September 1946, Discussing the Resettlement of Displaced Persons

**RESETTLEMENT
OF
DISPLACED PERSONS**

**MEMORANDUM
by
UKRAINIAN CANADIAN COMMITTEE**

[........]
British, American and French occupied forces in Europe are the *keepers* of approximately 800,000 refugees and displaced persons. These, the most unfortunate victims of war and resulting political conditions therefrom [........] are driven into despair and suicide by persistent pressure and threats of forceful repatriation.
[........]
While the permanent peace for the time being appears to be a remote possibility, depending on co-operation, goodwill and patient perseverance of all the powers and all the nations, proper solution and re-establishment

of displaced persons is exclusively in the hands and within possibility of the Western democracies.

[........]

As Canadians of Ukrainian origin, we are particularly and deeply interested in the future welfare of that portion of this group of displaced persons, numbering about 300,000, of Ukrainian nationality. They constitute a cross-section of sturdy, self-reliant sons of the soil, a better counterpart of that group of Canadians of Ukrainian origin who have proven their value as loyal and productive citizens of Canada within the last fifty years. Their tenacity, self-reliance, high moral standard, faith and devotion to Christian ideals has economic value and any country having empty spaces, seeking to develop its natural resources and increase its population by immigration can find no better opportunity than draw upon this particular group of people as a source of immigration. Their re-establishment, under the international body created for that purpose in any country climatically and politically suitable for free development creates no difficulty or unsurmountable problem. Given an opportunity and freedom they will rapidly establish and adapt themselves into the social and economic framework of any country as useful, loyal and productive element of their adapted land. No better proof or example for the above assertion can be found than the hundred thousands of Canadians of Ukrainian descent settled in Canada during the last 50 years, or the colonies of German refugees of Sudetenland, who came out together in 1939 and have grown into self-reliant and self-supporting settlements in Canada.

We therefore appeal to you, Sir, and to the Dominion Government, to initiate and create an international body of leaders of the Western democracies and assume the guardianship, salvation and re-establishment of displaced persons along the following or similar lines, namely:

(1) That suitable spaces open for settlement under favorable climatic, economic and political conditions be designated for re-settlement by the process of immigration of displaced persons.

(2) That transportation facilities and elementary needs for re-establishment be provided by international co-operation.

(3) That a favorable arrangement be made and a plan devised with several suitable countries to receive and absorb as immigrants a fair portion of [these] displaced persons.

As far as Canada is concerned, we feel that 300,000 of Ukrainian displaced persons could be easily absorbed by Canada, resulting in a wise and sound economic venture. We strongly feel that a substantial number of the prospective immigrants on their arrival in Canada will be taken care of by Canadians of Ukrainian origin, because of friendship and family relations. A large number of these immigrants could be absorbed in domestic service and industrial development of Canada as a whole, while the bulk will settle on the land and help utilize undeveloped natural resources of Canada into production and profit.

In conclusion, we wish to stress our deep conviction that an international body created for solution of the problem of refugees has immediate possibilities to carry such a plan through. The proposition is sound, logical, wise and possible of accomplishment. Removal of refugees from Europe will relieve the United Nations from the responsibility of maintaining them there in idleness and uncertainty, and will by itself solve to a large extent re-establishment of the native population in the after war reconstruction.

[........]

We again appeal to you, Sir, and the Government of Canada, to take the leadership in this regard.

Ukrainian Canadian Committee

Very Rev. Dr. B. Kushnir — *President*
J. W. Arsenych — *Secretary*

Source: Archives of Ontario,
G.R.B. Panchuk Collection

Presenting its views on the issue of postwar immigration policy, the Ukrainian-Canadian Left emphasized Canada's continuing need for agriculturists and labourers. They opposed the entry of professional classes and those who they felt were inimical to their interests. Paradoxically, the postwar immigration of Ukrainians, composed almost entirely of the labouring and farming classes, became a vehement opponent of the Ukrainian-Canadian Left.

No. 46: Brief Submitted to the Senate Committee on Immigration from the Association of United Ukrainian Canadians, Ukrainian Labour-Farmer Temple Association, and Workers' Benevolent Association, June 7, 1947, Concerning the Immigration of Ukrainians to Canada

BRIEF SUBMITTED TO THE SENATE ON IMMIGRATION ON JUNE 5th 1947

[........]

On May 29th, 1946, our delegation appeared before your Committee and presented a brief on the subject of immigration into Canada. In this our second appearance we wish to reiterate our support to a policy of broad immigration into Canada as beneficial to the interests and future welfare of our country and our position that such an immigration policy should exclude discrimination because of national origin or religious belief, particularly as it affects immigration of people of Ukrainian nationality.

[........]

We wholeheartedly concur with the recommendations of your Committee as published in the official report of the Debates of the Senate (March 11, 1947) and urge the quickest implementation of sub-sections (c) and (d) of Section 3.

(c) that surveys be undertaken immediately in Europe to determine the localities where immigrants may be found, and the conditions and anticipated problems to be met.

(d) that a survey be undertaken in Canada in order to determine the agricultural and industrial resources available for use by prospective immigrants, and the conditions and anticipated problems to be met.

Such comprehensive surveys, in our opinion, are the precondition for a consistent long-range immigration program for Canada, entirely apart from the temporary and narrower problems of permitting entry to relatives of Canadian residents and to *bona fide* "displaced persons" into Canada.

[........]

In carrying out Section 3, sub-section (d) of your Committee's recommendations, we propose that it be interpreted to include not only a survey of agricultural and industrial recources already under exploitation, but also the possibilities of opening new areas to cultivation and the initiation of new industries in Canada. The simple "dumping" of new farmers on areas already being cultivated or new workers in industries already staffed would neither offer the necessary inducement to immigrants nor to any extent increase our productive power, while it could have an unfavorable reaction on Canada.

We protest against the permission granted by Order-in-Council to groups and individuals to bring over contingents of workers from Europe on the basis of private "surveys" and selection and under conditions which smack of "indentured" labor and constitute a threat to employment and labor relations in our country.

[........]

We are of the opinion that, until the surveys recommended by your Commission and comprehensive measures of assistance to newcomers are undertaken by the government, Canada will continue to lack a positive and constructive policy for broad immigration.

During the past year there has grown a tendency in Canada to avoid facing the above fundamental problems in the working out of a genuine immigration policy and substitute therefore policies directly opposed to the successful solution of that issue.

Thus, instead of adhering to the fundamental policy of bringing in people of the laboring and farming classes, we now hear more and more about opening the gates to people of the professional and middle classes.

We submit that Canada's need for immigration arises from the need to enlarge our industrial and agricultural production, thus increasing our national income and the purchasing power of the Canadian people. This means that the basis of our immigration policy must be, (1) to bring in workers and farmers; and (2) to create conditions in Canada where they could engage in expanding industry and agriculture.

We believe that a proper survey would show that the need and possibility of placing professional classes in Canada is limited (and further complicated by the differences in language and educational standards of the people whom it is proposed to receive into Canada, making it necessary for lengthy re-education), and that under no circumstances should immigration from this source be permitted to substitute for the basic problem of worker and farmer immigration. This point was raised regarding doctors in Europe at the Health Committee of the Manitoba Legislature. It was agreed that professionals, graduating after Hitler came to power, have been trained and educated in Fascist ideology.

Similarly, under the phrase "selective immigration" there has grown a tendency to propose substitution of immigration of people of a particular religious or political background for a policy of broad immigration based on Canada's needs and perspectives.

We submit that this type of "selective immigration" is contrary to Canada's democratic traditions and in so far as it serves as a mask to cover the bringing over to Canada of the pro-Nazi remnants in Europe it is subversive and fraught with dangers to Canadian democracy and security.

If we are to adopt a policy of "selective immigration" on the basis of political record, then we suggest that in justice to the Canadians who sacrificed and died in the war the only acceptable immigrants should be those who fought against Nazi Germany and her satellites during the war and not those who fought with her against us and our allies.

Finally, there is the glaring preoccupation with the so-called "displaced persons" in Europe as a substitute for a genuine broad immigration policy.

In this regard we submit the following views:

1) Apart from the Jewish and Spanish anti-Fascist refugees the so-called "displaced persons" in and outside D.P. camps in Germany, Austria and Italy are either war criminals and Nazi collaborators who are wanted by the governments of their countries to stand trial or persons free to return to their homelands.

2) There is a long-standing decision of the Allied powers, further elaborated at the recent foreign ministers' conference in Moscow, to resolve this problem by handing war criminals over to their respective governments and repatriating the others to their homelands.

We are opposed to any policy which would make Canada a haven for war criminals or pro-Nazi politicians under the guise of "immigration".

We protest against the activities of certain agencies in Canada, which have been working to prevent the above proper solution of the so-called "displaced persons" issue by false propaganda both among the Canadian people and the "displaced persons" themselves. These activities were so scandalous that the British occupation authorities were compelled to ban entry of a number of Ukrainian-language newspapers *(Novy Shlyakh* and others) into their zone in Germany in June of last year. In April of this year the Allied control Council in Germany decided to disband all "Committee centres" and similar organizations operating against the interests of Allied powers among "displaced persons"; we would point out that many of these "centres" were organized from Canada and that the activities barred in Germany are still continuing from Canadian soil.

We urge that Canada's immigration policy be founded on the basis on which it was intended: the broadest recruitment of immigrants from the laboring and farming classes without prejudice or discrimination because of religion, creed or nationality, with government financing and assistance to place them where they would expand our industrial and agricultural production and contribute to the further building-up of Canada.

We thank you for your kind invitation to present our views.

Toronto, June 5, 1947.

SOURCE: Archives of the Association
of United Ukrainian Canadians

*Ukrainian refugees who arrived in Canada in the im-
mediate post-World War II period were proponents of a militant nationalism. Their political views put them at odds with
the established Ukrainian community in Canada.*

No. 47: Editorial, *Preserve Our Ties with Ukraine,* Гомін України
(Ukrainian Echo), *No. 1, December 15, 1948*

PRESERVE OUR TIES WITH UKRAINE

In its liberation struggle against the Russian occupier the Ukrainian
nation survives one of the most tragic of its historic periods. Our nation
must make many sacrifices in the often fatal contest with Russian imperialism — a contest which is already nearing its end. Foreseeing the impending catastrophe, Russia is putting forth all efforts to eliminate the
Ukrainian nation's revolutionary liberation movement, and to transform
Ukraine into a mere geographic entity. Russia is waging its continuous attack not only on the revolutionary elements, but on our language and
culture. Russia is now realizing the plan of widespread physical destruction of the Ukrainian nation. Continual mass arrests, executions, deportations of entire villages and countries, filling concentration camps in the
Russian north, periods of man-made famines in Ukraine — all of these
take from us not hundreds, thousands nor hundreds of thousands, but
millions of the greatest sons and daughters of Ukraine from among the
villagers, the laborers and the intelligentsia. And how many human
sacrifices were made by our nation during WWII when the *NKVD* herded
entire divisions consisting of Ukrainians, barely armed, into the range of
German bullets on the most dangerous areas of the front.

[........]

In light of the strengthened and concentrated Russian advance, as
well as those events which are before the Ukrainian community, new problems and responsibilities confront us. We must not only do all we can to
weaken the blows, but take advantage of all possibilities to impair the
strength of Russian imperialism.

It is in the interest of our liberation struggle to take advantage of all
opportunities to attack our enemy, weaken his position, mobilize all
freedom-loving forces against him.

[........]

For those of us who find ourselves in freedom outside the borders of
our homeland and do not directly participate in the fight with the occupier, it is our responsibility to continue our liberation fight with ap-

propriate methods and resources available to us in the countries of our temporary stay. We cannot, in lands not native to us, fold our hands and observe developing events. It is not enough to be inspired by the heroism of our Ukrainian insurgents. Ukraine does not need our tears, nor moving words of inspiration, but she demands of us active participation in the fight through every channel available to us. Every one of us carries with him — willingly or unwillingly — a certain amount of responsibility for the future of his nation and his homeland.

When we refer to these moments on the pages of our press, we are attempting to emphasize the ideas and positions for which our newspaper will stand. First and foremost, however, we strive to keep alive in the hearts of the Ukrainian diaspora a vivid picture of our struggling Ukraine so that we do not become wrapped up in the everyday burdens of the emigré community; so that no spiritual ties with the homeland are torn.

Over Ukraine, covered with blood, the apocalyptic horsemen continue to ride, leaving ruins behind them. Is it possible for us, even for a moment, to forget? Would it not be an unforgivable crime to withdraw from this fight when the entire nation with the remains of its strength, is fighting for its existence?

The situation demands that we preserve our ties with Ukraine!

SOURCE: *Гомін України*
(Ukrainian Echo), No. 1, December 15, 1948
[Translated from Ukrainian]

Faced with a Ukrainian Canadian Committee reinvigorated by postwar immigrants and the support of Canadian veterans of Ukrainian origin the government reviewed its relationship to this national body. Rather than involve themselves in international politics the authorities maintained that Ukrainians should integrate into Canadian society. The government would remain the sole arbitrator of Canadian foreign policy.

No. 48: Brief from the Ukrainian Canadian Committee to the Rt. Hon. Louis St. Laurent, Prime Minister of Canada, September 10, 1952, Discussing Political Matters which Concern the Ukrainian Canadian Community

[COPY]
BRIEF
CONCERNING THE UKRAINIAN CANADIAN COMMITTEE AND THE CANADIAN GOVERNMENT PRESENTED TO THE RIGHT HONOURABLE LOUIS S. ST. LAURENT, PRIME MINISTER OF CANADA

[........]

At this time the U.C.C. is striving to achieve the following purposes:

(a) The co-ordination and strengthening of the participation of the Ukrainian Canadian in Canada's efforts to promote the development of social and state organs and social life based on the Christian principles of civilization and democracy, on social justice and freedom, and on the sovereignty and the independence of nations,

(b) To act before governments and the citizenry of Canada as a mouthpiece of the just aspirations of the Ukrainian nation towards state independence on the ethnographic territories in Europe and from the standpoint of Canadian citizens to give the Ukrainian nation moral and financial aid directed towards the ultimate liberation of the Ukrainian nation from the foreign Russian communist subjugation and towards the restoration of the Sovereign and Indivisible Ukrainian State.

We are deeply convinced that these purposes stated in the constitution of the Ukrainian Canadian Committee have a wider meaning and can contribute to the constructive development of all phases of Canadian life. Consequently, for the general welfare of Canada, we, Canadians of Ukrainian origin, are applying and shall apply all our creative forces in peace and when required in war. These purposes were expressed by the three Ukrainian Canadian Congresses held in 1943, 1946 and 1950. The congresses were attended by a large number of delegates from all the Ukrainian democratic organizations in Canada and therefore without doubt these purposes can be regarded as the voice of the Ukrainian Canadians.

The Ukrainian Canadian Committee at this time humbly begs the Canadian Government to give consideration to our following requests:

1. The work of the Ukrainian Canadian Committee needs the continued moral support of the Canadian Government in the following respect, that the Government give recognition of the existence of the Ukrainian Canadian Committee as an authoritative representative body of the Ukrainian democratic group in Canada.

2. In relevant matters, especially those connected with the Ukrainian Canadians, it is urged that the Government seek the opinion of the Ukrainian Canadian Committee, in order to avoid possible undesirable mistakes.

[........]

3. In its present policy of championing the cause of the freedom of peoples, we ask the Canadian Government to make mention of the Ukrainians and a free Ukraine in international affairs and to give feasible support to the Ukrainian liberation movement and to the general movement to dismember imperialist Russia.

We also feel that the Canadian citizens should be informed through government channels of the possible relations of a free democratic Ukraine with Canada, particularly in trade and strengthening the block of democratic nations. Canadians must dispel the notion that the Ukrainian problem is an internal problem of Russia and that the Ukrainians are a Russian people. We believe it to be in the interests of Canada for the Canadian Government to treat the Ukrainian problem as part of the general problem of the freedom of all peoples from under the yoke of Russian tyranny and to prepare the Canadian people psychologically to understand it thus.

The Ukrainian Canadian Committee is doing everything possible within its means to bring about a clarification of the viewpoint in this matter. It needs the continued moral support of the government. We therefore beg of the Canadian Government that whenever its representatives make a declaration respecting the right of each nation to freedom to include among the names of such nations, also the Ukrainians. We also think that should Ukraine gain her freedom in the near future, the Canadian Government should anticipate such an event and be prepared beforehand to make a declaration of recognition of a free Ukraine, for such a gesture would have tremendous significance in bringing about favourable relations between the two countries.

The Ukrainian Canadian Committee on this occasion wishes to convey to the Canadian Government its deep gratitude for the inclusion of a Ukrainian section in the International Service of the CBC, known as the Voice of Canada. We extend our sincere thanks to the Minister of External Affairs, the Honourable L. B. Pearson, for the inaugural address at the opening of the program which disseminates information to 40,000,000 Ukrainians in the U.S.S.R. The Ukrainian Canadians are happy that Canada has in such a manner extended a friendly hand to the Ukrainian people. It is true that the 15-minute daily broadcast is very short but we hope that it will be possible to increase the daily time.

In reply to the Ukrainian language broadcasts of the Voice of Canada, the Soviet radio recently commenced a 30-minute daily broadcast to Canada from Kiev, the chief city of Ukraine. These Soviet broadcasts contain subversive communist propaganda, which should be appropriately counteracted by the Ukrainian Canadians over the network of the CBC. We are therefore making this request of the Canadian Government — to aid the Ukrainian Canadian Committee in its endeavours to

secure a "Ukrainian Hour" at least once a week over the Dominion network of the CBC (long-wave), which would be devoted primarily to
paralyzing communist propaganda from Kiev.

In presenting our requests to the Canadian Government, we feel con-
fident that consideration will be given to them and that we may expect
positive results.

Respectfully and humbly submitted,

UKRAINIAN CANADIAN COMMITTEE

Winnipeg, September 10, 1952

SOURCE: Department of External Affairs
(Canada), History Section, File: 10268 - 46

No. 49: Memorandum to R.C. Ritchie, Head of the First Political Division, Department of External Affairs, from J.A. McCordick, European Division, October 24, 1952, Commenting on the Recommendations in UCC Brief of September 10, 1952

October 24, 1952

SECRET

MEMORANDUM FOR MR. RITCHIE

Ukrainian Nationalism and the Ukrainian Canadian Committee

The Prime Minister's office referred to us a copy of a brief submitted
by the Ukrainian Canadian Committee to the Prime Minister when he
was in Winnipeg on September 10. The Prime Minister acknowledged
receipt of the brief in a letter dated September 23 and it would not appear
to be his intention to take up in detail with the Committee the points raised
in the brief.

2. It would not be in character for the Ukrainian Canadian Committee to refrain from further attempts to get the Government to accept their
"line" or at least some of it, and we should therefore be prepared to draft
replies to future submissions if asked to do so.

3. The brief submitted to the Prime Minister presents the familiar
Ukrainian nationalist case and we have, in fact, at various times formulated our attitude on the points in the brief. I think that the following
comments on several points in the brief represent the general feeling in the
Department.

4. On page 2 of the brief there are set out as (a) and (b) the two chief aims of the Ukrainian Canadian Committee. The first, which really concerns the integration of Ukrainians in Canadian life, is quite acceptable. The second, however, is not in accordance with Canadian policy. It reads as follows:

> To act before governments and the citizenry of Canada as a mouthpiece of the just aspirations of the Ukrainian nation towards state independence on the ethnographic territories in Europe and from the standpoint of Canadian citizens to give the Ukrainian nation moral and financial aid directed towards the ultimate liberation of the Ukrainian nation from the foreign Russian communist subjugation and towards the restoration of the Sovereign and Indivisible Ukrainian State.

5. It is not Canadian policy to support movements or organizations having as their aim the dissolution of the Soviet Union and/or the promotion of subversive activities in the territories of the Soviet Union, e.g. the Ukraine. This is not to say that in time of war or any other unforeseeable circumstances we might not decide to make an offer of independent statehood to the Ukrainians and/or other non-Russian minorities in the Soviet Union, but such decisions are for the future; for the present it would be unrealistic, dangerous and bad propaganda to adopt as Government policy the dismemberment of the Soviet Union or to give any encouragement to private organizations like the Ukrainian Canadian Committee which urged such a policy. Indeed, in the very different circumstances of war it might still be unrealistic to adopt such a policy, partly for the hardening effect it would have on the determination of the Great Russian people (cf. the effect of the "unconditional surrender" policy on the Germans) and partly because of the facts of history, geography and economics which led the historian W. E. D. Allen, who is sympathetic towards the Ukrainians, to conclude in his "The Ukraine" that:

> The fate of the Ukrainians becomes altogether a part of the obscure destiny of the nationalities at present under the rule of the Communist Government in Moscow. And the destiny of all these peoples must be a Russian destiny in the sense that the fluvial network of the Great Eurasian Plain is one geographical and economic whole out of which it is impracticable and would be unreal to attempt to carve separate and politically independent national units.

6. In view of the foregoing we would, I think, reject the requests listed in the brief. The first request is that some form of Government recognition be given to the Ukrainian Canadian Committee "as an authoritative representative body of the Ukrainian democratic group in Canada." Government recognition in the form requested is not given to private organizations in Canada.

7. The second request is that the Government consult the Ukrainian-Canadian Committee on all matters Ukrainian "in order to avoid possible undesired mistakes." This presumptuous proposal is quite unacceptable.

8. The third request is that the Government openly declare its support of the Ukrainian liberation movement and the movement to dismember the Soviet Union. The unacceptability of this request has been dealt with above.

9. Finally the Committee asks for Government help in arranging a weekly "Ukrainian hour" over the Dominion network of the CBC "which would be devoted primarily to paralyzing Communist propaganda from Kiev." I doubt if this request would be favourably received by the CBC, who probably share our reluctance to see special programmes of this kind become a feature of the Government-owned national broadcasting system.

[sgd.] J.A. McCORDICK
European Division

[Marginalia:] *The Ukrainian Canadian Committee are at*
it again. This is a good state-   C. A. RITCHIE
ment of the line we shall have to hold in
resisting their pressure.

I agree completely with the line   L. W.[ILGRESS]
taken in this memorandum.

SOURCE: Department of External Affairs (Canada), History Section, File: 10268 - 40

In 1949, the Canadian League for the Liberation of Ukraine was formed largely by post-World War II Ukrainian refugees. During the succeeding decade, its leading members wrestled with such questions as their relationship to the host society, role in Ukrainian-Canadian life and Ukrainian independence. Steadfastly, they insisted that their primary objective was to support the Ukrainian liberation struggle; they did not wish to expend their energies in a place where they felt Ukrainian aspirations could never be realized fully. However, they even-

tually joined the Ukrainian Canadian Committee and aban-
doned in practice if not in theory the idea of returning to
Ukraine.

No. 50: Minutes of 5th Conference of the Canadian League for the Liberation of Ukraine, 17-18 July, 1954, Discussing Organization's Objectives and Relationship to the Ukrainian-Canadian Community

MINUTES OF 5TH CONFERENCE

[.........]

W. Didiuk: [.........] The CLLU [Canadian League for the Liberation of Ukraine] across Canada has justified its existence, has grown and has earned itself the right of citizenship. The CLLU cannot be exclusively a political organization — it must be an organization for everyone and thus include various aspects of life and work, first and foremost, our youth and students. All community activities must be included in the concept of political activity. The membership of the CLLU must increase. Our political publications must be more widely circulated. But we should also not neglect English-language radio broadcasts which are of great importance. Women must be treated as equal partners, even when membership dues need to be paid. As for the UCC, we must do that which is most beneficial for our organization.

Y. Spolsky: [.........] It is a fact that we are experiencing a period of stagnation. We have made no progress for almost two years. We wasted potential opportunities in the beginning which today could have resulted in a membership numbering 10-20,000. We must find a way of rejuvenating enthusiasm and participation among our people. The main problem is to maintain a strong leadership. Our failures are a result of the fact that in the last five years we have had no new people in the National Executive — fresh blood which is equated with fresh ideas. We must completely change the methods we have practised to date, apply a more flexible policy, so as to easily approach the new generation, especially the youth already born here, mainly the students. We must work with the people, becoming active in Canadian political life. This participation still involves the obstacle of dual representation, but taking an example from our four MPs in Ottawa, we see that they are capable of presenting Ukrainian issues to a great number of Canadians. We must maintain close contact with them. It is also imperative that we break down the wall which separates us from the

UCC. Our lack of participation in the UCC has hurt us tremendously. Last year we tactically lost a campaign in this respect. Today we are capable of striking a bargain. The inactivity of our European centres, such as the Ukrainian National Council and the *OUN*, has also been a condition of our stagnation. We must influence these centres so that they, too, improve their positions.

M. Sosnowsky: [........] The CLLU must emphasize the area of external affairs, while in other areas of activity only a general plan of action is necessary. We will strengthen our influence only when we collectively participate in Canadian community and political life. In the inactivity of our European centres lies the threat of weakening the foundation of our nation's fight, which in turn could have a tragic influence on our work as a whole. We must ensure that this threat does not become widespread. W. Solonynka spoke against consolidation. This is an incorrect position. We must, at all costs, strive for consolidation, destroy the walls which separate us internally within the Ukrainian community. We must be at the centre of community life, and not standing at the sidelines criticizing. We must have a positive program, politics and approach. There is a psychological gap between us and the youth, specifically the students. We do not understand each other. We must agree on one acceptable concept and outlook, because otherwise they will never work with us. We are substantially losing biologically in Ukraine, whereas in Canada we are preserving our biological make-up. It is imperative that we prepare a program for our continued activity.

[........]

P. Bashuk: The speakers [have] presented a rather grim view considering the CLLU is only five years old. The situation is not as bad as portrayed. The work of the CLLU has not narrowed, it is possible that we have only drifted somewhat. Although the UCC issue has been discussed enough, we must realize that it is a reservoir of an already organized populace and we must take advantage of it. The UCC will be experiencing radical changes and we must take that into account when making any plans. The thought once posed by M. Sosnowsky in *Ukrainian Echo* "Homin Ukrainy" regarding the dominant role of Ukrainians in the Canadian prairies is worth noting.

* *
*

Following the discussion the following individuals spoke: Messrs. Deychakiwsky, Solonynka, Waranycia and Dr. Malaschuk. *P. Deychakiwsky* called the plans of Y. Spolsky utopia. *W. Solonynka* replied that he does not oppose consolidation but believes that the time is not yet right and the issue requires much more thought and preparation. Assimilation into

Canadian society is a natural tendency which cannot be fought. *Dr. Malaschuk* expressed his disappointment [........] that the main discussants spoke on issues which are unrealistic, and unnecessarily blew out of proportion the responsibilities of the CLLU, resulting in the defeatist comments about stagnation and so on. Thoughts about Switzerland in Canada are fantasies. We are not out to build a Ukraine in Canada. [........] Consolidation cannot be solely our goal, but it should be an instrument of our politics. We have a responsibility to increase our membership, and then our activities can be expanded. The CLLU has a future, because we are young, we are growing and we will continue!

SOURCE: Archives of the Canadian League for
the Liberation of Ukraine

In response to Ukrainian-Canadian pressure, the government produced an analytical document on why it did not accept the viability of the Ukrainian independence movement. The interpretation presented the Canadian government's case for maintenance of the international **status quo.**

No. 51: Confidential Memorandum from J. Léger, Under-Secretary of State for External Affairs to the Canadian Ambassador to the USSR, July 18, 1956, Clarifying the Views of Canadian Government on the Issue of Ukrainian Sovereignty

CONFIDENTIAL

July 18, 1956

MEMORANDUM FOR THE MINISTER

The Ukraine

From time to time the Canadian Government is subject to a certain amount of pressure by members of the Ukrainian-Canadian community who would like to see government policy statements and CBC IS broadcasts take a more forthright attitude towards the "liberation" of the Ukraine. A good example is the telegram you received on February 7 from the Ukrainian Canadian Committee seeking to interpret the Washington declaration as including the Ukraine, and requesting Ukrainians as among the peoples to be liberated. In this paper we propose to examine the validity of the proposition that the Ukraine can be considered a national political entity.

2. The historical Ukraine forms roughly the southern half of the great plain of European Russia, and is bisected into western and eastern halves by the Dnepr. By the XV century, Muscovy had emerged as the political and cultural centre of gravity in the northern half. The south-west (the western half of the Ukraine), had been drawn toward Poland by the XIV century, and was later absorbed into the united kingdom of Poland-Lithuania. From both these centres, the north and the south-west, but mainly from the latter, expansion took place to the south and east into the frontier zone *(Ukraina)* and over the lands of the modern Ukrainian SSR. The Ukrainian question originates in the distinct political and cultural development of the two regions from which the colonization of the Ukraine took place and in the fact that the south-western centre was largely responsible for the culture of the modern Ukraine.

3. In the south, Polish dominance bred continuous resistance under Ukrainian Cossack leadership. By the XVII century, Muscovite assistance had led to the defeat of the Poles, and, in return, by the Treaty of Andrussovo (1667), Muscovy acquired the eastern half of the Ukraine. This region was granted autonomy under a Cossack *hetman,* and there followed the Golden Age of the *hetmanshchina* [Hetman State]. The institution survived until 1764; but the gradual curtailment of local independence by Russian power began in 1708 [1709], when Peter the Great suppressed an effort by the *hetman* Mazeppa to win a wholly independent crown. Systematic Russification began under Catherine II; and Russia acquired the rest, the western half of the Ukraine, by the partitions of Poland, except for small territories in Galicia, Moldavia and Hungary. Nearly all of the Ukraine has thus been politically a part of Russia since the XVIII century.

4. As a result of its history, the Ukraine has many features with distinguish it from Russia proper. The language of the Ukraine derives from a Slavonic dialect spoken in the western half in the XI century. More significant differences from the Russian of Muscovy appeared between the XII and XIV centuries, and its vocabulary came to be distinguished by the large number of words borrowed from Polish. From its beginnings, it has been less influenced than Russian by Old Church Slavonic (which is to the Slavonic languages what Latin is to the Romance languages), and is therefore more "popular". By the XVIII century, Ukrainian was very largely a distinct language: today, it differs from Russian as much as

broad Scots from the tongue of southern England. The Ukrainian Church is closer to the people and far less authoritative than the Russian. The religious experience of the region includes the influence of Rome, which was entailed in polonization, and which culminated in the establishment of a Uniate Church in 1569, that is a church following the Orthodox rite but acknowledging the supremacy of the Pope. The Ukrainian is more rural than the Russian, and his agricultural institutions were never as coercive. Although the great cities of the region played a leading role in the capitalist and industrial development of Russia, this development was dominated by urban Russians of the Ukraine; and large estates, wage labour and progressive farming in the western half accounted for much of the surpluses of grain exported by Russia in the XIX century.

5. Kiev, the capital of the Ukraine, is, of course, one of the oldest cities of Russia and one of its cultural and historic centres, but the sad fact is that today it contains almost as many Russians as Ukrainians. Odessa was founded relatively recently and was from the outset largely populated by Russians and Jews. Kharkhov, its biggest industrial centre, lies on the ethnic boundary and is also largely Russian. Therefore, the purely Ukrainian parts of the republic are mostly the backward agricultural areas and small towns.

6. The Ukrainian nationalist movement developed as a consciousness of a distinct cultural unity, and never achieved a mature political expression. The region is celebrated for its cheerful songs and attractive folklore. Some of this is Slavonic (pre-Polish) in origin, but its most vital element stems from the Cossack revolts against Polish influence in the XVII century. The anti-Roman Catholic struggle of this period first made the Ukrainians aware of their nationality and gave them their early national literature. The Ukrainian movement began as a provincial and dilettantesque interest in the tradition enshrined in this literature, and burgeoned in the XVIII century with that literature. Yet the peasantry remained passive, and the bulk of the gentry turned increasingly to Moscow for preferment. Although in the first half of the XIX century, the movement acquired a more nationalist and political form, yet the Ukrainian revolutionaries of the latter half still exhibited no marked nationalist tendencies. By 1905, the movement had spread to the countryside, and it appeared, despite persecution during the First World War, that the Ukrainian people might indeed be ready to make an effective demand for independence.

7. In March 1917, representatives of the region demanded autonomy and their council was recognized by the Kerensky Government in August. Following the Bolshevik Revolution in October, the Ukrainian Council proclaimed an Ukrainian People's Republic [Ukrainian Democratic

Republic], the independence of which was accepted in principle by the Bolsheviks.

8. In February 1918, Germany and Austria signed a separate peace treaty with officials of the Ukrainian People's Republic and agreed to provide the Ukraine with manufactured goods in return for grain. Following pressure by the Bolsheviks, the Kiev government appealed to the Central Powers for assistance; German and Austrian troops thereupon occupied the Ukraine and established their own puppet government. With the collapse of the Central Powers, the puppet government was overthrown and this was followed by a period of turbulence and fighting between Ukrainian, Polish, Bolshevik and White Russian forces. In 1920, with Soviet Russian troops occupying the Ukraine, Russia and Poland concluded the Treaty of Riga by which both recognized Ukrainian independence [Ukrainian SSR]. In December 1920, a Russo-Ukrainian treaty was signed defining relations between the two Soviet republics, the net result of which was to establish permanent control over the Ukraine by the Soviet Government in Moscow.

9. Following the rise of Stalin the Soviet Government carried out a gradual policy of Russification in the Ukraine, and its dominance was intensified by purges during the 1930's. As a result, in World War II, Ukrainians in large part welcomed and facilitated the rapid advance of the German army, and this period was characterized by wholesale desertions and the surrender of army units. The Nazis, however, failed to capitalize on the pro-German sentiments of many Ukrainians, though, in spite of the stupidity of their policy, they were able to raise an Ukrainian formation to fight the Soviet Union. After three years of German occupation, the Ukraine was reoccupied, and the activities of large numbers of Ukrainians was used by the Soviet Government to justify increasing postwar Russification and a policy of resettlement particularly in Central Asia for large numbers of Ukrainians.

10. The campaign for an independent Ukraine has been carried on vociferously by intensely nationalistic emigré groups abroad. They generally detest the Russians and regard Soviet communism as an incidental manifestation of the old Russian imperialism. They also deplore the probability that, even if the eastern European satellites were liberated, the Ukraine would still find itself a province of the USSR. The Ukrainians in Canada who are most militant, appear to be a small though conspicuous minority of the Ukrainian Canadians.

11. While there is undoubtedly a cultural background to support the Ukrainian claim to independence, there is only a relatively slender case to be made on economic grounds. In an objective view, it seems very doubtful that the modern Ukraine would be a viable entity, if wholly divorced from the USSR; and, in view of this fact, it seems probable that Ukrainian

nationalism, if it secured its way, would not ultimately demand more than an honestly federal solution.

12. So far as political grounds are concerned, the Ukrainian nationalist interpretation of the original alliance with Moscow (that this was purely and solely a military alliance between equals) cannot be substantiated; the Ukrainian nationalist movement never achieved completely mature political expression; the Ukrainian people were never organized in a completely independent state; nor was an Ukrainian state ever recognized by any power other than Poland.

13. I think that you will agree that we should welcome, in our broadcasts and public statements, any tendency toward the liberalization of the Soviet regime. One possible aspect of this tendency, which would be very welcome to Ukrainians, would be the evolution of a more genuinely federal relationship between the Ukrainian SSR and the USSR. We might give subtle encouragement to this idea by reference to Canada's federal solution to a bi-national problem.

14. The political evolution of the Slavic peoples of Russia has been extremely slow, and it may be a tragic truth that Ukrainian nationalism was only reaching a maturity which could no longer be ignored, when it was nipped in the bud by the Bolshevik Revolution. There would appear to be, however, no justification under present circumstances for the Canadian Government to include the Ukraine among those nations under Soviet domination whose claims to national independence and freedom we endorse. Canada was, of course, a co-signatory with the Ukraine of the United Nations Charter, but the opinion of the legal experts is that this fact cannot be construed as indicating Canadian recognition of the independence of the Ukrainian SSR.

15. While you were in Europe, Mr. Drew made a speech in favour of Ukrainian nationalism at a rally in Winnipeg, and implied that, "peaceful liberation" of the satellites, which he endorsed, should include the Ukraine. This question may therefore become of increasing importance during the coming months.

16. I strongly recommend that the Canadian Government should not commit itself either directly, or indirectly through CBC IS broadcasts, to the liberation of the Ukraine as an objective of Canadian policy. Apart from the futility of such a policy, I strongly doubt that, even in the unlikely event that the communist regime in Russia should disappear, an independent Ukraine would be a practical possibility. We would, in any case, seriously offend all Great Russians by advocating such a policy.

17. I should be grateful if you would let me know if you agree that our statements on the Ukraine should continue to avoid this issue, if possible, and concentrate on expressions of sympathy with Ukrainian cultural sur-

vival and the hope that its national spirit and traditions will not be swamped in the communist tide.

JULES LÉGER

SOURCE: Department of External Affairs, (Canada), History Section, File: 10268 - 40

Encouraged by Cold War developments, representations were made to Canadian officials by Ukrainian-Canadian nationalist delegations. These petitions were casually dismissed, although never overtly so, despite assurances that their views would be noted.

No. 52: Memorandum to J. Léger, Under-Secretary of State for External Affairs, from J. Watkins, European Division, Department of External Affairs, November 6, 1957, Commenting on an Audience with the Ukrainian Delegation which Presented a Brief on the Question of the Liberation of Ukraine

CONFIDENTIAL

November 6, 1957

MEMORANDUM FOR THE UNDER-SECRETARY

Ukrainian Delegation

At four o'clock this afternoon the Minister received a delegation of twelve from the Canadian League for Ukraine's Liberation. Nine were from Toronto, two from Ottawa and one from Sudbury. The Minister agreed to allow the photographer accompanying them to take his picture with the group. They had also been received by the Minister of Labour.

2. The spokesman of the delegation, Mr. Frolich, after congratulating the Minister on his election, referred to the pamphlet they had published, entitled "The Policy of Liberation as an Aspect of Canadian Foreign Policy," a copy of which the Minister had received, and said that in their opinion, the Western Powers were not exploiting sufficiently in their

policies and propaganda the vulnerability of the Soviet Union as a multi-national state. He quoted a remark of Mr. Khrushchev's to Mr. Reston of the *New York Times* as evidence of Soviet anxiety on this score, and expressed the hope that more advantage could be taken of this weakness, especially, of course, in respect of the Ukraine.

3. The Minister mentioned that in his first speech at the United Nations, on the occasion of Malaya's admission, he had contrasted the United Kingdom's policy of transforming colonies into nations with the reverse policy followed by the Soviet Union. Regarding a "liberation" policy, however, he could not quite recall when it had last been advocated, perhaps it was in a speech by Mr. Dulles about two years ago. Silence from the Ukrainians. The Minister noted the danger of arousing false hopes of assistance and illustrated this from his experience of Hungarian refugees at the University of Toronto who were bitter about the deceptive impression created, in their opinion, by *Voice of America* broadcasts to Hungary before the revolution.

4. When the Minister asked to be instructed in the history of the Ukraine as an independent state, Mr. Frolich avoided any reference to its over three hundred years of union with Russia and concentrated on the brief span of independence beginning with the Russian revolution in 1917, and ending with the incorporation into the Soviet Union in 1919 or 1920.

5. The Minister inquired about Ukrainian acquaintances in Winnipeg and Toronto, thanked the delegation for their courtesy in calling, and assured them that their views would be noted. He managed to make them all feel important, which as far as I could judge, was the main object of their visit.

[sgd.] J.B.C. WATKINS

SOURCE: Department of External Affairs, (Canada), History Section, File: 10268 - 40

The continuing attempts of the Ukrainian Canadian Committee to play a role in influencing Canadian foreign policy led officials to compile information on this body. The document notes divisions within the postwar immigration and also a profound split between them and prewar Ukrainian immigrants.

No. 53: Confidential Memorandum from the Director of the Citizenship Branch to the Deputy Minister of Citizenship and Immigration, May 1958, Describing Weaknesses of the Ukrainian Canadian Committee

CONFIDENTIAL

WEAKNESSES OF THE UKRAINIAN CANADIAN COMMITTEE

(a) **Financial Weakness**

Since the Committee has no provision for individual membership, its finances are entirely dependent on the annually assessed payments made by member organizations.[........]

As a result, the salaries of the permanent staff of the U.C.C. are low and acceptable only to former displaced persons and not to established Ukrainian Canadians. The limited knowledge of the English language among permanent staff members makes it necessary for them to conduct the official correspondence of the U.C.C. mainly in Ukrainian.

The fact that most of the headquarters' staff of the U.C.C. consists of recent political refugees, moreover, has led to the manifestation of a European-oriented political attitude in much of the Ukrainian language printed matter emanating from the U.C.C. Thus considerable stress is placed on events behind the Iron Curtain, on the threat of Russian world domination, and on the claims of the Ukrainian nation for self-determination and independence.

(b) **Influence of Newcomer Organizations**

The inclusion of a number of national organizations whose membership consists entirely of post-World-War II immigrants, in the Ukrainian Canadian Committee in 1953, has tended to bring in an element with more European than Canadian interests and ties.

These organizations are:

Ukrainian National Democratic League
Carpatho-Ukrainian War Veterans League
Ukrainian Technical Society
Ukrainian Democratic Youth Association
Ukrainian Association of Victims
      of Russian Communist Terror
Ukrainian Plast Association
Canadian Friends of Liberation of Ukraine.

The new tendency was reflected in the composition of delegates to meetings of the "Wider Council" and their pressure to give European Affairs more attention. During the sessions they took a great deal of time, insisting on discussions of European affairs while other members waited impatiently to discuss current business matters of the U.C.C. [.......]

The U.C.C. refused to accept as members, the extreme nationalist wing of refugees-immigrants, the "League for the Liberation of the Ukraine" and its strong youth group — who are now in their 30'ies — the "Ukrainian Youth Association" *(S.U.M.)*. Thus the U.C.C. does *NOT* represent *ALL* anti-communist Ukrainian organizations.

Due to a definite tendency among established Ukrainian Canadians in *Eastern Canada* to lose interest in their ethnic organizations, the actual membership of the nominally strong provincial branches with their many member organizations has been declining. As a result, the majority of active members in Eastern Canada are now post-Word-War II immigrants. In Western Canada, however, although the provincial branches are apparently weaker, having fewer member organizations, the active membership of established Ukrainian Canadians has been maintained. The western branches of the U.C.C. are therefore stronger than the eastern ones and also more representative of the Canadian-Ukrainian point of view, rather than of the point of view of the European refugees.

SOURCE: Public Archives of
Canada, RG 26 Vol. 66, File: 2-5-4

While prepared to accept the presence of the Ukrainian Soviet Socialist Republic at the United Nations, Canadian officials, in their communications to foreign representatives, emphasized that this status did not imply formal recognition of Ukraine's sovereignty. Ukraine could only be considered to be a constituent part of the Soviet Union.

No. 54: Confidential Letter from J. Fournier, Department of External Affairs, to D. Hay, High Commissioner of Australia, December 20, 1961, Concerning the Canadian Attitude on the status of Soviet Republics Including Ukraine

[COPY]

Ottawa, December 20, 1961

CONFIDENTIAL

Dear Mr. Hay,

In connection with our conversation of this morning, I think you may be able to use the information set out below concerning the Canadian attitude to the Soviet Republics.

Byelorussia and the Ukraine

The Canadian attitude to recognition of Byelorussia and the Ukraine was defined in the House of Commons on May 17, 1954, by the then Parliamentary Assistant to the Secretary of State for External Affairs, replying to a question. The question and reply were as follows:

> **Question:** *Does Canada recognize Byelorussia and the Ukraine as separate and sovereign states or only as integral states of the USSR?*
>
> **Reply:** *Canada does not recognize Byelorussia and Ukraine as separate and sovereign states, but regards them as constituent parts of the USSR. However, Canada, in common with other members of the United Nations, accepted Byelorussia and the Ukrainian Soviet Socialist Republic as members of the United Nations when the organization was formed in 1945.*

It is clearly implied in the above that our acceptance of Byelorussia and the Ukraine as members of the United Nations does not constitute the extension to them of any degree of recognition as sovereign states. The opinion of our Legal Division, given in connection with another problem, is that a vote by Canada in favour of the admission of a state to the United Nations does not involve recognition of that state.

[........]

If I can give you any other information on this or other subjects, I would be glad to do so.

Yours sincerely,

JEAN FOURNIER

His Excellency D.O. Hay, D.S.O., M.B.H.
   High Commissioner for Australia
      90 Sparks Street
         Ottawa

SOURCE: Department of External Affairs
(Canada), History Section, File: 6126 - 40

Characterizing the nature of the Ukrainian Soviet Socialist Republic's constitutional status as specious, Canadian officials also rejected the validity of Ukrainian nationalist claims.

No. 55: Confidential Memorandum from N. Robertson, Under-Secretary of State for External Affairs, to the Secretary of State for External Affairs, January 15, 1962, Outlining Canada's Attitude to Ukrainian Nationalism

CONFIDENTIAL

January 15, 1962

MEMORANDUM FOR THE MINISTER

CANADIAN ATTITUDE TO UKRAINIAN NATIONALISM

Attached is a copy of an article from the Edmonton Ukrainian-language newspaper "Ukrainski Visti" of December 11, 1961. The article alleges that there are differences between the views which you and the Prime Minister have expressed in public about Ukrainian independence and those which are actually held by the Department. The article contends that the Government could prove its belief in the idea of Ukrainian independence by recognising the Soviet Ukraine as a sovereign state, which, under the Soviet Constitution, it claims to be.

2. I understand that the Prime Minister has seen a copy of this article, and I think it likely that the Canadian Ukrainian community will approach him before long on this subject. He might therefore like to have the Department's views. My own preliminary thoughts are set out below; if you wished, I could have these points put in a memorandum to the Prime Minister.

1) Article 18 (a) of the Soviet Constitution says that the Ukraine is empowered to conduct its own external relations. This article was added in 1944 in order to strengthen the argument that the Ukraine and Belorussia were entitled to seats in the United Nations. To attach importance to the article might be to encourage the Russians to claim seats for the other 13 republics, also empowered, under Article 18 (a), to conduct their own external relations.

2) The Constitution says that the Soviet Union is a Federation with divided powers, and carefully divides governmental re-

sponsibility between the central and regional governments. In fact, however, the Soviet system is not a federal one because policy on all matters is made, and its execution supervised, by the Communist Party, which, in theory as well as in fact, is directed from the centre. The Communist Party is mentioned only once in the Soviet Constitution, not in this context.

The Constitution, therefore, is in this way as in many others not followed in practice. To extend diplomatic recognition to the Ukraine on the strength of the Ukraine's constitutional autonomy would be to give the Soviet Constitution a responsibility it does not deserve.

3) If we extended diplomatic recognition to the Ukraine, we would (I think) be the first country, communist or not, to do so. As far as I know there are no foreign diplomatic missions in Kiev or Ukrainian diplomatic missions abroad. There are some foreign (all communist) consular missions in Kiev. In about 1948, the U.K., probably seeking to make a propaganda point, enquired about an exchange of diplomatic missions with the Ukraine. It received no answer and has never revived the question.

4) Except for a brief period during 1917-1919, mostly under a German puppet regime, the Ukraine has had no separate national existence since the 17th century. During most of that period it has been partitioned among Russia, Poland and Austro-Hungary. The Ukrainian nationalist movement is of fairly recent origin (19th century) and has had a mainly literary expression through the poet Taras Shevchenko and his followers. Spoken Ukrainian is a dialect of Russian about as different from Russian as lowlands Scots is from London English. During the 19th century, however, a literary Ukrainian was evolved by the nationalists mainly so that written expression could be given to nationalist aspiration.

5) It is hard to know how much nationalist sentiment persists in the Ukraine. The literary groups which carried the nationalist banner in the 19th century are gone. It is doubtful if the Kiev intelligentsia now thinks on political matters much differently from its Moscow counterpart. In the countryside, especially in the Western Ukraine, there is probably some fairly vigorous anti-Russian, anti-Communist, anti-Government feeling. But this is a different matter from the Ukrainian nationalism we know and is common to the rural populations of all the non-Russian areas of the USSR.

6) The German occupation probably dealt a serious blow to Ukrainian nationalism by bringing home to Ukrainians the fact that there were tyrannies worse even than Stalin's, and that the Ukraine needed a protector. Postwar improvements in life throughout the Soviet Union may have reinforced this lesson to the advantage of the Russians.

7) It is worth noting that many Ukrainians have risen to high office in the Party and Central Government not only in Kiev but also in Moscow. (Like the Scots in London!) The most obvious example is Khrushchev who, although he was born in a village just outside the Ukraine, has a Ukrainian name and speaks Ukrainian. Many other examples could be found.

8) E. N. Carr, a foremost authority on Soviet history, has pointed out in his *Bolshevik Revolution* that after the revolution, the Ukrainian national movement had little support either from the peasants or from the industrial workers. This was because it had failed to advocate even mild social reform, and because the economic interdependence of Russia and the Ukraine had been generally recognized. These weaknesses opened Ukrainian nationalism to a variety of foreign pressures and deprived it of any freedom of action. "Its final bankruptcy," concludes Carr, "came in 1920 when its last active leader, Petlyura, made his pact with the Poles, the national enemies of the Ukrainian peasant."

3. While for the above reasons there seems to be real difficulty in dealing with the Ukraine on the basis of its "political individuality," this does not prevent our dealing with those aspects of the Ukraine problem which might come under human rights provisions. Although the Russians would no doubt oppose such interference under Article 2 (7), which prohibits raising questions "essentially within the domestic jurisdiction of any state," there is an argument that the Ukraine, as a founding member of the Organization, could be said to have "sovereign equality" with all members, including the U.S.S.R. However, the very strong reaction to be expected from the Soviet Government should not be overlooked.

[sgd.] N. A. ROBERTSON

SOURCE: Department of External Affairs (Canada), History Section, File: 6126 - 40

Selected Bibliography

M. Gulka-Tiechko, "Inter-war Ukrainian Immigration to Canada, 1919-1939." (Master's thesis, University of Manitoba, 1983).

J. Kolasky, *The Shattered Illusion: The History of Ukrainian Pro-Communist Organizations in Canada.* (Toronto: Peter Martin Associates, 1979).

B. Kordan, "Disunity and Duality: Ukrainian Canadians and the Second World War." (Master's thesis, Carleton University, 1981).

M. Kostash, *All of Baba's Children.* (Edmonton: Hurtig Publishers, 1977).

L. Luciuk, "Searching for Place: Ukrainian Refugee Migration to Canada after World War II." (Doctoral dissertation, University of Alberta, 1984).

M. Lupul (ed.), *A Heritage in Transition: Essays in the History of Ukrainians in Canada.* (Toronto: McClelland and Stewart Ltd., 1982).

O. Martynowych, "Village Radicals and Peasant Immigrants: The Social Roots of Factionalism among Ukrainian Immigrants in Canada: 1896-1918." (Master's thesis, University of Manitoba, 1978).

M. Marunchak, *The Ukrainian Canadians: A History.* (Winnipeg-Ottawa: Ukrainian Academy of Arts and Sciences, 1982).

B. Panchuk, *Heroes of Their Day: The Reminiscences of Bohdan Panchuk.* Edited by L. Y. Luciuk (Toronto: Multicultural History Society of Ontario, 1983).

J. Petryshyn, *Peasants in the Promised Land: Canada and the Ukrainians, 1891-1914.* (Toronto: James Lorimer and Company, 1985).

J. Rozumnyj, et al., (eds.), *New Soil — Old Roots: The Ukrainian Experience in Canada.* (Winnipeg: Ukrainian Academy of Arts and Sciences, 1983).

F. Swyripa, *Ukrainian Canadians: A Survey of Their Portrayal in English-Language Works.* (Edmonton: University of Alberta Press, 1978).

F. Swyripa and J. Thompson (eds.), *Loyalties in Conflict: Ukrainians in Canada during the Great War.* (Edmonton: Canadian Institute of Ukrainian Studies, 1983).

P. Yuzyk, *The Ukrainian Greek Orthodox Church in Canada, 1918-1951.* (Ottawa: University of Ottawa Press, 1981).